Understanding Workplace Harassment

Lori McDowell

HR PRACTITIONERS' SERIES

© 1997 Thomson Canada Limited

All rights reserved. No part of this publication may be reproduced, stored in a retrieval system, or transmitted, in any form or by any means, electronic, mechanical, photocopying, recording, or otherwise, without the prior written permission of the publisher.

The publisher is not engaged in rendering legal, accounting or other professional advice. If legal advice or other expert assistance is required, the services of a competent professional should be sought. The analysis contained herein represents the opinions of the author and should in no way be construed as being official or unofficial policy of any governmental body.

Canadian Cataloguing in Publication Data

McDowell, Lori, 1960-
 Understanding workplace harassment

(HR practitioners' series)
Includes bibliographical references and index.
ISBN 0-459-56325-4

1. Harassment in the workplace — Canada. 2. Sexual harassment — Canada. 3. Personnel management — Canada.
I. Title. II. Series.

HF5549.5.M5M32 1997   658.3'145   C97-931331-7

One Corporate Plaza, 2075 Kennedy Road, Scarborough, Ontario M1T 3V4
Customer Service:
Toronto: (416) 609-3800
Elsewhere in Canada/U.S. 1-800-387-5164
Fax (416) 298-5082
Word Wide Web: http://www.carswell.com
E-mail: orders@carswell.com

Table of Contents

Preface v

Acknowledgements vii

About the Author ix

What is Harassment? 1

Who is Covered? 19

Where are People Protected? 29

Is this Harassment? 35

Who is Responsible? What are the Consequences? 45

What Can Be Done About It? 55

What are the Basics of a Harassment Policy? 69

What are Other Organizations Doing? 77

How to Investigate? 103

What Do the Human Rights Commissions Say? 113

Appendix — Canadian Legislation 137

References 143

Index 145

Preface

Workplace harassment has become a buzz phrase of the nineties. Employers, employees, unions, boards of inquiries, arbitration boards and courtrooms spend an inordinate amount of time dealing with the issues surrounding harassment. There are reams of judicial decisions, media publications and commentaries focusing on its aftermath. However, an understanding of harassment and its consequences, both in the workplace and in employees' personal lives, is not as commonplace.

This book reviews the various forms harassment can take, as well as who, how and where they are protected. Several examples of harassment are offered, including the difficult issues of e-mail, dating, jokes and posters. Its consequences are also covered, with the appropriate responses an employer must take if confronted with an allegation of harassment.

The steps that can be taken are explored, including the basic elements of constructing an in-house harassment policy. Several examples of working policies are given.

Finally, investigation tips are reviewed and the last word is given to Canada's human rights commissions, most of whom have published their own guidelines and fact sheets on harassment.

Acknowledgements

I would like to thank the people and organizations who have helped me produce this book. Several human rights commissions and other organizations across Canada have provided excellent information for their constituents on harassment issues. I thank them for their perseverance in what for many commissions and organizations must be a time of dwindling resources and cutbacks. I am also grateful to those organizations that gave me their generous permission to quote from their publications.

Lelean Boer has been instrumental in helping me complete this book. Her assistance, organizational skills and tirelessly positive attitude have been invaluable.

I also wish to thank Derry McDonell at Carswell for his patience and Patricia Wee, my editor at Carswell, for her review of this material and her many helpful suggestions.

Finally, I thank my family — my husband Vic and my children, Alex and Amy, for their support while I wrote this book. Vic and Alex encouraged me to start and then, with perhaps even more enthusiasm, to finish this manuscript. Amy insisted on taking a more literal "hands-on" approach, often sitting with me at my computer while I attempted to explain once again what it was that I was writing about and why she couldn't help me type. Her incomprehension that it should take so long to write about "treating people fairly" was telling.

About the Author

Lori McDowell, LL.B., is a human rights pension and benefits consultant with Coles Hewitt, a major benefits and human resources consulting firm in Vancouver, British Columbia. Her specialty is advising employers, employees and unions on human rights, accommodation and diversity issues in the workplace.

Lori has been with Coles Hewitt since 1993. In all, she has been providing consulting services in the field of employee benefits, pensions and human rights issues for 10 years. She started her career in private practice with a law firm.

Lori is a past Vice-Chair of the Corporate Counsel Subsection and of the Pension and Benefits Subsection of the Canadian Bar Association, B.C. Branch. She was also the Chairperson of the Canadian Pension and Benefits Institute (Pacific Region).

She is the author of the book, *Human Rights in the Workplace*, and editor of the newsletter, *Employers' Human Rights & Equity Report*, both published by Carswell.

CHAPTER ONE

What is Harassment?

INTRODUCTION

It has often been said that if we could just answer the question — "What *exactly* is harassment?" — we would be much closer to eliminating the problem. However, in what is perhaps the most difficult part of dealing with workplace harassment, an all-purpose, exhaustive definition is elusive, if not impossible.

The general definition of "harassment" is unwanted behaviour based on a protected ground, such as sex or race, that has a negative impact in the workplace. The behaviour can include a broad range of conduct from physical contact to eye contact. Both the case law and the legislated definitions are general. For example, in Ontario, the *Human Rights Code* defines harassment as "engaging in a course of vexatious comment or conduct that is known or ought reasonably to be known to be unwelcome". In Manitoba, harassment is defined to mean:

s. 19(2) In this section, "harassment" means

(a) a course of abusive and unwelcome conduct or comment undertaken or made on the basis of any characteristic referred to in subsection 9(2); or

(b) a series of objectionable and unwelcome sexual solicitations or advances; or

(c) a sexual solicitation or advance made by a person who is in a position to confer any benefit on, or deny any benefit to, the recipient of the solicitation or advance, if the person making the solicitation or advance knows or ought reasonably to know that it is unwelcome; or

(d) a reprisal or threat of reprisal for rejecting a sexual solicitation or advance.

The laws against harassment in each human rights Act in Canada have been included in the Appendix to this book.

One of employees' most often asked questions, however, continues to be — just what action or behaviour is included? Some guidance may be offered about the type of behaviour that may constitute harassment, but there is no definitive list of conduct or words. This certainly can cause great frustration for employees faced with what they feel to be ever-changing rules in the workplace. It can also lead to a demeaning of harassment issues as bewildered employees walk away from workplace training sessions on harassment awareness wondering if they had better not even speak to their fellow employees anymore. In this scenario, everyone loses.

Some behaviour should always ring warning bells, such as any physical interaction of a sexual or racist nature, regardless of the surrounding circumstances. But the line can become blurred once conduct moves beyond the physical to the verbal or visual. Some guidance may be offered.

For example, a quick and admittedly simplistic self-test is for employees to ask themselves a simple variation of the golden rule — "How would I feel about this type of behaviour being directed at me?" This self-test can also help an employee to determine whether the conduct could be unwelcome.

While some behaviour is offensive and inappropriate in the workplace, how did it become illegal discrimination? One of the early cases dealing with sexual harassment compared the problems associated with harassment with other workplace issues and said, why not? If the law is active in other employment-related issues, why would it not be involved to protect people from harassment as well?

> There is no reason why the law, which reaches into the workplace so as to protect the work environment from physical or chemical pollution or extremes of temperature, ought not to protect employees as well from negative, psychological and mental effects where adverse and gender-directed conduct emanating from a management hierarchy may reasonably be construed to be a condition of employment. (*Bell v. Ladas* (1980), 1 C.H.R.R. D/155 (Ont. Bd. of Inquiry, Shime), at page D/156)

Some human rights commissions, unions and employers have provided lists of examples of harassing behaviour. These are not intended to be exhaustive lists of unacceptable behaviour; rather, they provide a context within which people can evaluate behaviour. The following are the most frequently identified types of conduct:

1. Physical
    - assault
    - touching, patting, pinching
    - massaging
    - caressing
2. Verbal
    - comments or jokes that demean or belittle another individual
    - comments about a person's body
    - comments about another's ethnic origin, race or colour

- negative stereotyping
- comments about sexual attractiveness, *or* about sexual unattractiveness
- comments about sexual desires or practices

3. Visual
   - posters or calendars that could be offensive
   - lewd looks — elevator eyes, staring at body parts.

The safest way to avoid offending another employee is simply to not engage in questionable behaviour. If in doubt, *don't* do it.

WHAT IS SEXUAL HARASSMENT?

Sexual harassment is any unwelcome sexual behaviour or behaviour based on sex that affects the workplace in a negative way. Sexual harassment is the most common type of workplace harassment. It can affect both men and women, but women are most often the target.

Sexual harassment includes a broad range of behaviour, from unwanted physical contact to comments, gestures, looks and pictures. It includes not only the "slap and tickle" version of harassment, and the "sleep with me and you'll get the promotion" type of harassment, but also comments and jokes based on sexual stereotypes. This latter form of harassment is often known as gender harassment and is reviewed below under "What is Gender Harassment?".

Several of the human rights Acts across Canada provide different definitions of sexual harassment. The Ontario and Manitoba definitions of sexual harassment are referenced above in the Introduction. In Nova Scotia there is yet another definition in the human rights legislation:

s. 3(o) "sexual harassment" means

> (i) vexatious sexual conduct or a course of comment that is known or ought reasonably to be known as unwelcome,
> (ii) a sexual solicitation or advance made to an individual by another individual where the other individual is in a position to confer a benefit on, or deny a benefit to, the individual to whom the solicitation or advance is made, where the individual who makes the solicitation or advance knows or ought reasonably to know that it is unwelcome, or
> (iii) a reprisal or threat of reprisal against an individual for rejecting a sexual solicitation or advance.

The Newfoundland *Human Rights Code* definition is short and to the point:

> s. 2(g) "harass" means to engage in a course of vexatious comment or conduct that is known or ought reasonably to be known to be unwelcome.

The Newfoundland section is identical to the one contained in the Ontario Code.

Yet another definition exists in the *Canada Labour Code* which governs all employees working in federally regulated industries such as banks and transportation and communication companies. It provides:

> Sec. 247.1 In this Division, "sexual harassment" means any conduct, comment, gesture or contact of a sexual nature:
>
> (a) that is likely to cause offence or humiliation to any employee; or
> (b) that might, on reasonable grounds, be perceived by that employee as placing a condition of a sexual nature on employment or on any opportunity for training or promotion.

The definitions in the human right legislation vary widely but do share some common elements about what can constitute sexual harassment. For example, each definition is broad enough to include these characteristics:

1. It can encompass many types of behaviour, including both physical and verbal conduct.
2. It has a sexual component or is based on the gender of the recipient.
3. It is unwelcome.
4. It occurs in connection with the employee's work.
5. It has a negative impact on the workplace.

Some Canadian jurisdictions (such as British Columbia) do not include a definition of sexual harassment. However, the courts have filled this vacuum.

Bell v. Ladas (1980), 1 C.H.R.R. D/155 (Ont. Bd. of Inquiry), the first judicial case in Canada dealing with sexual harassment, involved two waitresses and their manager. Cherie Bell and Anna Korczak were waitresses at the Flaming Steer Restaurant for a brief period. They each quit and claimed they had been propositioned by the manager.

The chairperson of the board of inquiry, Owen Shime, set out the framework in which harassment allegations should be reviewed. He focused on the power imbalance and stated:

> Discrimination based on sex is prohibited by the Code. Thus, the paying of a female person less than a male person for the same job is prohibited .... But what about sexual harassment? Clearly, a person who is disadvantaged because of her sex is being discriminated against in her employment when her employer denies her financial rewards because of her sex, or exacts some form of sexual compliance to improve or maintain her existing benefits. The evil to be remedied is the utilization of economic power or authority so as to restrict a woman's guaranteed and equal access to the workplace, and all of its benefits, free from extraneous pressures having to do with the mere fact

that she is a woman. Where a woman's equal access is denied or when terms and conditions differ when compared to male employees, the woman is being discriminated against.

The forms of prohibited conduct that, in my view, are discriminatory run the gamut from overt gender-based activity, such as coerced intercourse to unsolicited physical contact to persistent propositions to more subtle conduct such as gender-based insults and taunting, which may reasonably be perceived to create a negative psychological and emotional work environment. There is no reason why the law, which reaches into the workplace so as to protect the work environment from physical or chemical pollution or extremes of temperature, ought not to protect employees as well from negative, psychological and mental effects where adverse and gender-directed conduct emanating from a management hierarchy may reasonably be construed to be a condition of employment. (at page D/156)

In another case, *Janzen v. Platy Enterprises Ltd.*, [1989] 1 S.C.R. 1252, 10 C.H.R.R. D/6205, the Supreme Court of Canada set the rules for sexual harassment that now apply in all cases. Diana Janzen and Tracey Govereau were waitresses in Manitoba at The Pharos Restaurant, owned by Platy Enterprises Ltd. Both complainants alleged sexual harassment by the restaurant's cook, Tommy Grammas.

Janzen worked at the restaurant from August to October 1982. Shortly after starting work, Grammas made several unwelcome sexual advances towards her including touching her. Janzen repeatedly objected to his behaviour; however, he continued for over a month. Once the overtly sexual conduct stopped, Grammas continued to make the work environment difficult for Janzen by refusing to cooperate with her food orders and generally treating her poorly. Janzen complained to the restaurant manager who told her she was overreacting and that nothing could be done to change the cook's behaviour.

Govereau was also a waitress at the restaurant. She worked there for only two months, from October to December 1982. During her first week of employment, Grammas kissed her on the mouth. Govereau objected time and again to Grammas' behaviour but he did not stop. She also complained to the manager and the physical harassment stopped shortly afterwards. Again, however, the cook's physical behaviour was simply replaced by unjust criticism of her work and verbal abuse. Govereau was soon fired.

The Supreme Court of Canada found that the common element among all definitions of sexual harassment was:

> ... the concept of using a position of power to import sexual requirements into the work place thereby negatively altering the working conditions of employees who are forced to contend with sexual demands. (at page D/6225)

It found that sexual harassment could take many different forms. The court stated:

Sexual harassment is not limited to demands for sexual favours made under threats of adverse job consequences should the employee refuse to comply with the demands. Victims of harassment need not demonstrate that they were not hired, were denied a promotion or were dismissed from their employment as a result of their refusal to participate in sexual activity. This form of harassment, in which the victim suffers concrete economic loss for failing to submit to sexual demands, is simply one manifestation of sexual harassment, albeit a particularly blatant and ugly one. Sexual harassment also encompasses situations in which sexual demands are foisted upon unwilling employees or in which employees must endure sexual groping, propositions and inappropriate comments, but where no tangible economic rewards are attached to involvement in the behaviour. (at page D/6226)

The court then added its own definition of sexual harassment in one of the most important judicial comments that has ever been made about sexual harassment:

Without seeking to provide an exhaustive definition of the term, I am of the view that *sexual harassment in the workplace may be broadly defined as unwelcome conduct of a sexual nature that detrimentally affects the work environment or leads to adverse job-related consequences for the victims of the harassment* .... When sexual harassment occurs in the workplace, it is an abuse of both economic and sexual power. Sexual harassment is a demeaning practice, one that constitutes a profound affront to the dignity of the employees forced to endure it. By requiring an employee to contend with unwelcome sexual actions or explicit sexual demands, sexual harassment in the workplace attacks the dignity and self-respect of the victim both as an employee and as a human being. (at page D/6227, emphasis added)

The court also commented that while either sex can be harassed, it usually would be women who are victims because of the typical structure of the workforce:

Perpetrators of sexual harassment and victims of the conduct may be either male or female. However, in the present sex-stratified labour market, those with the power to harass sexually will predominantly be male and those facing the greatest risk of harassment will tend to be female. (at page D/6227)

Of course, men can also be subjected to sexual harassment. Any unwelcome behaviour based on sex qualifies, regardless of who is the source or recipient of the behaviour. This includes employees or others harassing members of the same or opposite sex by requesting sexual favours, groping, leering or making sexual suggestions or comments.

In yet another case, *Romman v. Sea-West Holdings Ltd.* (1984), 5 C.H.R.R. D/2312 (Can. H.R. Comm.), a male deckhand complained of sexual harassment by the male captain. The tribunal said that this was sexual harassment. The tribunal stated:

It should never be part of a person's employment environment, or part of their employment situation, to have to submit to the touching of the genitals. That must be seen as unacceptable. Nobody should have to put up with that as part of having a job. It is clear from the evidence that Mr. Romman in no way welcomed these advances or promoted them. He reported them to the owner of the tug and made it clear that these advances were unwelcome and worrisome. In my opinion, there is a duty upon the owner being so informed to put an immediate stop to such practises. His failure to do so would render him liable for damages under the human rights legislation. (at page D/2314)

WHAT IS GENDER HARASSMENT?

Conduct that does not have a sexual element to it but is based on gender can also be considered sexual harassment. Often, this behaviour consists of jokes and comments based on negative or rigid stereotypes about gender, such as what is "women's work", or what is a "man's job". This type of harassment is often called gender harassment rather than sexual harassment to distinguish it from harassment that has sexual overtones.

Other examples stem from the fact that women bear children, or from outdated notions of who is the "weaker sex". This can be a difficult form of harassment to address because it is often based on outdated ideas of chivalry or old-fashioned paternalistic ideals. It can occur because someone is, in their own mind, being considerate when they refuse to allow a woman to lift heavy objects when that is part of her job, or deny a man an opportunity because a job involves cleaning which is "women's work".

In one case, *Broadfield v. De Havilland/Boeing of Canada Ltd.*, (1993), 19 C.H.R.R. D/347 (Ont. Bd. of Inquiry), Christine Broadfield was hired to work as a bench and structural assembler at De Havilland/Boeing of Canada Ltd. After working in this capacity for about two months, she was asked to become a supervisor in her area. At the time, she was advised that she would be the first female supervisor at the plant and might encounter some resistance from her co-workers.

After accepting the position, Broadfield was subjected to anonymous, abusive telephone calls at her home. At work she was sent pornographic pictures and was the subject of gender-based obscenities and threats. In spite of the abuse, her employer maintained a "hands-off", neutral policy towards the incidents. Broadfield eventually complained that she was being sexually harassed at work.

A human rights board of inquiry heard her complaint. It stated that although most claims of sexual harassment involved sexually-oriented comments or conduct, it was also recognized that gender-based conduct could constitute sexual harassment. The board stated:

> Most claims of sexual harassment have to do with sexual solicitation, sexually-oriented comments or actual contact of a sexual nature. However, it has been recognized for more than a decade that harassment because of sex also includes "more subtle conduct such as gender-based insults and taunting".... That is the nature of the complaint in this case: Ms Broadfield alleges that her right to freedom from harassment in the workplace has been infringed because her gender has caused her fellow employees to create a poisoned or hostile working environment which her employer has not taken adequate steps to correct. (at page D/366)

The board agreed with Broadfield that the behaviour that she had encountered was sexual harassment.

In another case, *Burton v. Chalifour Bros. Construction Ltd.* (1994), 21 C.H.R.R. D/501 (B.C. Human Rights Council), a female carpenter-lather had been employed in the construction business for 11 years and had complained of sexual harassment by her co-workers. Karen Burton was the only female employee on the construction site. She was subjected to posters of nude women in the lunchroom and verbal abuse. She complained about the conduct and it worsened. She was shunned by her co-workers and began to be concerned about her physical safety as a result of some comments and behaviour exhibited by several of her co-workers.

Statistical evidence was introduced at the hearing that only 3 per cent of the construction industry employees were female. This number had remained constant since the 1970s. The Council took note of the fact that although more women were entering the trades, more women were also leaving.

Burton's employer, Chalifour Bros. Construction Ltd., conceded that the conduct to which she had been subjected was harassment, but argued that its response to her complaints was sufficient to avoid an award being made against it. The Council Member found that the employer had not taken appropriate steps to address Burton's complaints, and stated:

> . . . employers have a responsibility to maintain a workplace free of discrimination. An employer's failure to respond quickly and effectively to a complaint of harassment may increase the remedial consequences to the employer by perpetuating the discriminatory environment. (at page D/505)

Some employers have begun reviewing the issues of gender harassment apart from sexual harassment. Often, professions or occupations that have traditionally been in the male domain can be rife with gender harassment. For example, the legal profession, once a male bastion, has had its ranks significantly increased with female lawyers. This has prompted a review of the relative position of women in the profession.

In 1993, The Canadian Bar Association Task Force on Gender Equality in the Legal Profession presented the issues of gender harassment in fairly strong terms. The findings are not necessarily unique to the legal field and some of their comments are reprinted here:

One of the instrumental causes of gender discrimination against women is, of course, the male attitude toward women. It is often expressed in the form of cherished convictions as to the proper role of women. In spite of the fact that men also have children and are sexual beings, there is a tendency to regard all women in relation to their biological and/or sexual function. Such stereotyping is a major barrier to access and advancement in the profession.

The arguments most often put forward to explain or excuse discrimination are summarized as follows:

- that women's careers are likely to take second place to bearing and raising children. The profession is a secondary role for them.
- that women are less intelligent and less capable than men or because of their manner and psychology, are less suited to a career in an adversary system.
- that women are less acceptable to clients than men.
- that women have equal opportunities but fail to take full advantage of them.

Each of these assumptions reflects a failure to treat women as individuals who, like men, have a number of options open to them at various stages of their careers from which they will make choices according to their personal wishes and priorities. Education about the nature of sexual harassment and stereotyping should alleviate some of the attitudes which underlie this conduct. Men must learn to think of women lawyers as lawyers first, and as women second.

Reprinted by permission of The Canadian Bar Association.

This developing area of harassment surprises some employees. Many employees are familiar with the notion of harassment involving sexual activity or at least sexual discussion. Many others, however, are not as familiar with the idea that sexual or gender harassment can involve the repetition of age-old, and badly outdated, notions of the role of women and men in society.

This is one area where impressive gains can be made in dealing with harassment simply by informing employees that they are protected from such behaviour. The idea that unwelcome comments are not only inappropriate but also against human rights laws can be a welcome relief for some and a source of surprise to others. Care must be taken however to introduce this idea with some measure of sensitivity for those who have perhaps engaged in such behaviour unwittingly.

Many employees will have to be specifically told that comments based on gender stereotypes are unwelcome and inappropriate. The notion of gender harassment is relatively new and employees should be expected to adhere to the rules once they understand them, not before.

WHAT IS RACIAL HARASSMENT?

Racial harassment, one element of racism, is seen as a symptom of a deeply embedded problem. In a decision on jury selection, the Ontario Court of Appeal commented on racism at all levels of Canadian society:

> Racism, and in particular anti black racism, is a part of our community's psyche. A significant segment of our community holds overtly racist views. A much larger segment subconsciously operates on the basis of negative racial stereotypes. Furthermore, our institutions, including the criminal justice system, reflect and perpetuate those negative stereotypes. These elements combine to infect our society as a whole with the evil of racism. (*R. v. Parks* (1993), 15 O.R. (3d) 324 (C.A.) at page 342, leave to appeal to S.C.C. refused (1994), 28 S.C.R. (4th) 403 (note))

Racial harassment is unwelcome conduct based on a person's race, colour, ancestry, national, ethnic or place of origin that affects that person's workplace in a negative way. It is demeaning, humiliating or degrading behaviour inflicted on an employee, when acting within the scope of his or her employment duties, by a co-worker, supervisor, client, customer, supplier, or another.

Harassment on the basis of any of the terms making up racial discrimination, including one's race, colour, ancestry, nationality, ethnic background or place of origin, offends against human rights legislation. This is the case even though racial harassment is not mentioned in most of the human rights statutes (see the Appendix for the wording of each statute). As with sexual harassment, the prohibition against racial discrimination that has developed in the case law is interpreted as prohibiting racial harassment as well. As a result, racial harassment is against the law regardless of whether it is actually referenced in the relevant human rights statute.

The same principles that apply to sexual harassment apply to racial harassment. The definition of harassing behaviour, the boundaries of the workplace, the appropriate response and the notion of employer liability are all applicable in the same way to racial harassment as they are to sexual harassment.

The legal definition of what constitutes racial harassment is broad. Examples of the types of behaviour that have been held to be racial harassment will help provide more concrete details. They include:

- racial slurs;
- name-calling;
- racist jokes;
- negative stereotyping;
- physical assault, pushing, shoving;
- bullying;

- threats;
- demeaning pictures, posters and graffiti.

The numerous cases of racial harassment provide graphic examples of the types of behaviour that will constitute racial harassment. Most of such behaviour consists of name-calling, derogatory comments, and racist slurs and jokes. In one case, a long-time employee received a written document entitled, "Job Application for Niggers" through inter-office mail. In another case, a complainant was fired for swearing at a customer who had sworn first at her, calling her a "f— Hindu who should never have been hired to work in a public-related service". (*Hinds v. Canada (Employment & Immigration Comm.)* (1988), 10 C.H.R.R. D/5683 (Cdn. Human Rights Trib.); and *Mohammad v. Mariposa Stores Ltd.* (1990), 14 C.H.R.R. D/215 (B.C. Human Rights Council).)

In another case, an employee's supervisor and co-workers had referred to him, a Fijian, as "little toby," "black man," "chocolate," "buckwheat," "boop" (apparently slang for Bhupinder, a common Indian name), "joe boy" and "our token black boy". The employee's supervisor testified that all of this was simply in good fun. The board of inquiry that heard the case disagreed and said that the name-calling was racial harassment. (See *Ram v. McDonald's Restaurants of Canada Ltd.* (1991), 16 C.H.R.R. D/70 (B.C. Human Rights Council).)

The impact of verbal abuse and racial taunts and jokes can be devastating for the individuals who endure them. In the *Hinds* case, the board of inquiry noted the impact of the written material the complainant received:

> The effect of this kind of racial slur can never adequately be understood by anyone who has not experienced it first hand. It strips away a person's dignity and destroys his sense of self-worth in a way that may be irreparable .... this offensive act seriously affected his self-respect and went to the core of his very well-being. (*Hinds v. Canada (Employment & Immigration Comm.*), *supra*, at page 82)

Also, the comments and conduct need not be directed at the complainant. They can be directed at another individual's race or even directed toward another race in general. In one case of racial harassment, the board of inquiry stated:

> According to this jurisprudence, which I accept as relevant for the present case, Ms. Lee would find herself in an adverse environment if indeed racial slurs and other untoward practices occurred, *even if such discriminatory practices were not directed against herself.* It remains therefore a question of factual evidence to establish whether such incidents did occur and if they did... the Code was offended. (*Lee v. T.J. Applebee's Food Conglomeration* (1987), 9 C.H.R.R. D/4781 (Ont. Bd. of Inquiry, Plaut) at page D/4783)

Racial harassment of an employee can involve the blatant abuse of an individual because of his or her skin colour or something more subtle but just as inappropriate. For example, singling out members of a particular race for demeaning treatment even where the treatment itself does not focus on the individual's race can be racial harassment. The fact that only the members of one group are the constant butt of jokes, even non-racial jokes, can be an example of harassment.

In 1994, the Ontario Human Rights Commission published a Policy Statement on Racial Slurs and Harassment and Racial Jokes. The Policy Statement outlines the Commission's position on racial slurs, jokes and harassment based on one's race, ancestry, place of origin, colour, ethnic origin, citizenship and creed. It provides some guidance in this developing area, including where comments or actions are not directed toward a particular individual. This portion of the Statement gives some good examples of the types of behaviour that would be considered harassment:

> [The] equality provisions of the Code may be breached by racial slurs or actions which are not directed toward a particular individual but nonetheless adversely affect the environment for that individual. Examples include the following:
>
> i) Demeaning racial remarks, jokes or innuendoes about an employee, client or customer, or tenant told to other employees, tenants, clients or customers
>   - may impair the right of those persons who are the subject of the comments to be viewed as equals and create a "them/us" barrier.
> ii) Racial remarks, jokes or innuendoes made about other racial groups in the presence of an employee, tenant or client
>   - may create an apprehension on the part of members of other racial minorities that they are also targetted when they are not present.
> iii) The displaying of racist, derogatory or offensive pictures, graffiti or materials
>   - is humiliating and also impairs the right of those persons who are members of the targeted racial group to be viewed as equals.
> iv) Racial remarks, jokes or innuendoes about an employee, client, or tenant or about the racial group of which they are a member, which are stated to or in the presence of a non-racial minority person
>   - may cause discomfort on the part of the non-racial minority person and may have the effect of creating an environment where the opportunity for beneficial inter-racial interaction is lost or impaired.
>
> In the above or similar situations, the conduct at issue must be objectively evaluated. It must be of such a nature and degree so as to amount to a denial of equality through the creation of a poisoned environment.
>
> © Queen's Printer for Ontario, 1994.
Reproduced with permission.

Harassment on the basis of race may now require a more sophisticated understanding of harassment than earlier cases where obvious discriminatory conduct involved physical or direct verbal conduct. While some cases still involve blatantly unwelcome comments, others involve more subtle ostracizing. The level of sophisticated knowledge will continue to evolve as people's understanding and sensitivity toward peoples of other cultures and countries grows. Again, this is where education is critical to provide employees with an opportunity to avail themselves of this evolving area. The development of a harassment policy that is introduced in conjunction with a solid, non-threatening education program is critical to help avoid a workplace environment with racial harassment.

WHAT IS MENTAL AND PHYSICAL DISABILITY HARASSMENT?

Disability is a protected ground under each human rights Act in Canada. Several jurisdictions use different language to refer to the same thing — some use "handicap" and some differentiate between physical and mental disabilities, but the coverage for employees is the same. Whether stated or not, each Act protects employees from harassment on the basis of any disability. The same rules that apply to sexual harassment or harassment on any other grounds will also apply to harassment on the basis of one's physical or mental disability. Harassment on the basis of a disability is a violation of an employee's human rights. (See the Appendix, Canadian Legislation, for the wording for each jurisdiction.)

Employees with mental disabilities face unique challenges because of the very nature of their disability. "Equality for All", a 1985 report of the Parliamentary Committee on Equality Rights, included this passage from the Canadian Mental Health Association:

> Mental illness is one of the least understood and least accepted of all illnesses. It creates fear and stereotypical responses in people. Yet who are the mentally ill? Potentially they can be people who suffer from varying degrees of illness, from short term situations that temporarily incapacitate an individual to long term illnesses that require continuous support and attention. Psychiatric disabilities have many possible causes, sometimes physical, sometimes psychological and sometimes social. For a great many people, such illnesses are shameful and embarrassing and as a result they are very reticent to stand up for their rights or to protest when injustice has been done to them. (cited in *Battleford and District Co-operative Ltd. v. Gibbs*, [1996] S.C.J. No 55, at paragraph 13).

While there are few cases of mental disability harassment, one, *Boehm v. National System of Baking Ltd.* (1987), 8 C.H.R.R. D/4110 (Ont. Bd. of

Inquiry), provides a good example of what should not happen. In *Boehm*, the complainant was subjected to verbal abuse by his foreman who called him "dummy" and "stupid". The foreman also unjustifiably criticized his work in front of other employees and continually threatened to fire him.

The board of inquiry looked at the actions of the supervisor and the effect of harassment on an employee with a mental disability:

> Mr. Woods (the supervisor) was cruel and mean toward Mr. Boehm in his treatment of him. In this case, as I have said, the offending supervisor was aware that his conduct and comments were unwelcome. Having said that, I add that I do not think Mr. Woods intended Mr. Boehm to have the severe mental anguish he did. Mr. Woods intended to annoy him, to put him down and to hurt him. This is enough to constitute harassment. (at page D/4122)

Regarding employees with mental disabilities, the board noted that extra care may have to be taken to avoid offending them. The board said:

> However, I add as an obiter that, in my view, where a disabled person is an employee, there is an obligation upon the supervisor not to use even relatively innocuous conversation which might not offend non-disabled persons, if such conversation can be reasonably perceived to be hurtful to the disabled employee. That is, the sensitivity of the disabled employee must be reasonably accommodated. (at page D/4122)

Another case, *Ghosh v. Domglas Inc.* (1992), 17 C.H.R.R. D/216 (Ont. Bd. of Inquiry), reviewed a situation in which teasing an employee about his limp became harassment on the basis of his physical disability.

Ashit Ghosh worked for Domglas or 18 years. In April 1982, Ghosh was injured in an accident at work. This left him with a noticeable limp. Ghosh said that after his accident, his supervisor and other employees of Domglas taunted him about the way he walked.

The employer had argued that the comments were simply observations or statements that might have been intimidating, but were not harassment. The employer said Ghosh was being unreasonable in his perception of the behaviour. The board disagreed and found that the comments and conduct were "alarming, dismaying, frightening or daunting" and therefore could be harassment.

The board also found that, even if the employees were unaware that their conduct towards Ghosh was unwelcome, they ought to have known it. The board said that the proper test for imputing knowledge to the other employees was whether reasonable people similarly disabled would find the conduct to be unwelcome and, if so, whether reasonable people in the respondent's position would know that to be the case. The board decided that any reasonable disabled person would not have welcomed the conduct and that any reasonable employees should have known that.

> I have no doubt that any reasonable person inflicted with a similarly conspicuous limp resulting from an injury sufficiently painful to affect his ability to continue to perform his former duties would not welcome being the object of frequent derisive comments suggestive of a condition feigned to secure financial and workplace advantages. Nor do I doubt that reasonable persons not so disabled would know that to be so .... The reasonableness of the subsequent actions taken by Mr. Ghosh because he found it vexatious has no bearing on whether the respondents ought to have known their conduct to have been unwelcome when they indulged in it. Indeed, no overt action by the victim is necessary in order for it to be concluded that a reasonable person would know that the conduct was unwelcome. The conclusion that a respondent ought reasonably to have known the conduct to be unwelcome is not precluded by the fact that its victim suffered in silence. (at page D/223)

The board found that the taunting Ghosh had endured was harassment on the basis of his disability.

Harassment on the basis of one's disability, be it physical or mental, is perhaps a surprising new development in the human rights field for many employees. Employees with a comfortable understanding of what constitutes sexual harassment may be floored by the fact that teasing a co-worker about a limp, a nervous tic or a stutter would be a similar violation of the co-worker's rights.

Again, this is an area in which most employees can benefit from a good education program at the time a workplace harassment policy is introduced or amended. The facts about disability harassment are an eye-opener and can go a long way toward preventing workplace harassment in this area before it starts.

WHAT IS RELIGIOUS HARASSMENT?

Employees are also protected from harassment on the basis of their religion. Federal employees as well as those employed in Manitoba, Ontario, Quebec and Newfoundland are specifically protected from harassment on the basis of their religion because of the wording in their human rights statutes. Some of these jurisdictions also define "harassment" for their domain and some provide a defence for employers. (For the complete wording of each human rights law in Canada, see the Appendix.)

Employees in the remaining provinces and territories are also protected from harassment on the same basis that they are protected from any form of discrimination in employment. Each statute in Canada protects employees from religious discrimination and the courts have interpreted discrimination to include harassment even where the laws do not specifically mention harassment.

Religious harassment generally takes the form of verbal abuse, joking or taunting an employee about his or her religious beliefs, comments about religious practices whether real or imagined by the harasser, voiced perceptions about people with similar religious beliefs or comments about religious attire or headgear.

This protection extends to religious beliefs that an employee does *not* have as well. One case involved the owner-managers of a firm who identified themselves as born-again Christians. Religious posters and stickers were displayed in the workplace. The managers made negative comments about other religions to the employees and criticized their personal behaviour. With the exception of one employee, the employees were not interested and began to feel uncomfortable with the extent of pressure being exerted on them. The employees complained of harassment on the basis of religion. The board of inquiry agreed that this behaviour on the part of the managers was religious harassment.

The development of a harassment policy should include time spent reviewing the implications of each potential area of harassment. Although most employees are aware that comments related to another's religious beliefs can be inappropriate, they may not have attached the label "harassment" to them. This is even more the case when comments about another's clothing, headgear or ceremonies are taken into account. Employees must understand that comments about religion and religious practices are harassment just as comments about someone else's sexuality are harassment. Again, education and information are critical first steps. When a policy or a change to a policy is introduced, employees' attention should be drawn to each one of the protected grounds, including religion.

WHAT IS SEXUAL ORIENTATION HARASSMENT?

Harassing employees because they are gay or lesbian is discrimination on the basis of sexual orientation and is prohibited by the human rights laws. Employers, managers and unions who participate actively in harassment or who do nothing to stop it can also be guilty of discrimination.

Sexual orientation harassment may take the form of gay-bashing, jokes, expressed opinions based on negative stereotypes, name-calling or pictures.

In one case, an insurance company president referred to an employee he knew to be lesbian as "Mister" and commented about her use of cologne and her clothing. The employee was later fired. The employee complained to the Human Rights Commission that she had been discriminated against on the basis of her sexual orientation. The board of inquiry that heard the case agreed and awarded damages from not just the company, but also from the president personally for the discriminatory comments he had made. (See

Waterman v. National Life Assurance Co. of Canada (No. 2) (1993), 18 C.H.R.R. D/176 (Ont. Bd. of Inquiry).)

Also, employees can be harassed by comments based on a sexual orientation other than their own. For example, an employee can be harassed by a co-worker's comments about gays even though the employee himself is not gay. The harassment does not have to be direct, that is, about the individual employee. Accordingly, knowing that a colleague is heterosexual does not mean that it is acceptable to tell that employee jokes about gays and lesbians. A heterosexual employee can also be harassed by these comments.

Employers are responsible for ensuring that all employees are free from harassment of any kind in the workplace. Because an employee's sexual orientation is not always obvious, it is helpful for employers and unions themselves to emphasize that gay and lesbian employees are included in the protection of a workplace harassment policy.

WHAT IS AGE HARASSMENT?

Harassment on the basis of age is relatively unknown. Nonetheless, it could still pose a problem if employees are unaware of the implications of some of their actions regarding another employee's age. Age harassment includes unwelcome behaviour based on age that leads to negative consequences in the workplace.

Typical examples of age harassment involve comments and jokes about advancing age. For example, constant references to an employee's age, particularly if they were linked to the employee's ability to continue to do a job, could be harassment on the basis of age.

Discussions with employees on this front inevitably lead to a review of birthday celebrations and pranks. Every workplace seems to be able to recall a birthday gift or card that may have crossed the boundaries of good taste. The question then becomes "was that harassment?" The answer can be yes. However, there are two points to bear in mind. First, was it a one-time occurrence and second, was it tied to the employee's ability to perform his or her job. Often, in the case of age harassment, the remarks or visual images are confined to the moment. To constitute harassment, it is likely that a pattern of similar remarks or visual images would be required. Not a lengthy pattern, however, but certainly more than an isolated incident. The pattern would be strengthened considerably if the employee's abilities were also called into question on the basis of age. For example, if the comments were made by a supervisor that "old seniors like you can't do this sort of work" to a firefighter or someone else in a physically demanding job, age harassment could be established.

Age harassment is a new and, as yet, undeveloped area. Informing employees that this is an area where some sensitivity is in order and providing them with some examples of the forms of age harassment may be sufficient to prevent it from occurring.

WHAT IS PERSONAL HARASSMENT?

Personal harassment consists of unwelcome comments or actions that demean or humiliate an employee. Unlike all the other forms of harassment, the comments or actions do not need to be based on any of the protected grounds, such as age, sex or race. Personal harassment is abusive, inappropriate behaviour that is nasty, but not discriminatory.

One workplace harassment policy defines personal harassment as:

> objectionable conduct or comment, directed towards a specific person, which serves no legitimate work purpose and has the effect of creating an intimidating, humiliating, hostile or offensive work environment.

Examples of behaviour that would fit within this definition include:

- threats, bullying, coercion;
- actual or threatened physical assault;
- verbal assault, taunting or ostracizing;
- malicious gestures or actions.

Each of the other forms of harassment is given mandatory protection under the human rights statutes of each Canadian jurisdiction. Personal harassment however is not. No employer is required to protect its employees against rude and abusive behaviour that is not also discriminatory. Employers are only expressly required to protect their employees against inappropriate behaviour that is based on sex, age, race, religion, disability and in most jurisdictions, sexual orientation.

In fact, many employers choose not to deal with personal harassment. Many are concerned that opening up the policy to deal with personal harassment will take away from its main focus, which is to prevent or manage human-rights-related harassment. Many others are worried that they could be subjected to a large number of complaints if they enable employees to complain about generally inappropriate or abusive behaviour.

Many employers have, however, chosen to protect their employees against any kind of harassment, whether it is covered by a protected ground or not. This allows employers to deal with personality conflicts, bad management styles and other workplace issues within the harassment policy framework. These employers prefer to deal with the issues within a formal process, with trained employees designated to deal with all forms of harassment.

CHAPTER TWO

Who is Covered?

JOB APPLICANTS

Employees are not the only group that is protected from harassment in the workplace. Job applicants, whether they are ultimately successful or not, are also protected from harassment that could occur during the course of the application, interview and testing process. Even if the applicant is not ultimately successful, he or she is entitled to this protection. Any actions that would be harassment to a regular employee would be considered harassment toward a prospective employee.

A typical example of harassment in the interview process would be questioning an employee about sexual activity. Less obvious examples could include inappropriate questioning regarding the applicant's plans to have children, their age, marital status or religion.

Employers must be careful to steer clear of personal questions and to focus on the job requirements. Several human rights commissions in Canada have prepared guides to assist employers with interviewing. The chart below was prepared by the Canadian Human Rights Commission. It includes some of the questions that may legally be asked of job applicants and also provides examples of questions that are illegal.

A GUIDE TO SCREENING AND SELECTION IN EMPLOYMENT

SUBJECT	AVOID ASKING	PREFERRED	COMMENT
NAME	about name change: whether it was changed by court order, marriage, or other reason maiden name		ask after selection if needed to check on previously held jobs or educational credentials

A GUIDE TO
SCREENING AND SELECTION IN EMPLOYMENT

SUBJECT	AVOID ASKING	PREFERRED	COMMENT
ADDRESS	for addresses outside Canada	ask place and duration of current or recent address	
AGE	for birth certificates, baptismal records, or about age in general	ask applicants if they are eligible to work under Canadian laws regarding age restrictions	if precise age required for benefits plans or other legitimate purposes, it can be determined after selection
SEX	males or females to fill in different applications		during the interview or after selection, the applicant, for purposes of courtesy, may be asked which of Mr/Mrs/Miss/Ms is preferred
	about pregnancy, child bearing plans, or child care arrangements	can ask applicant if the attendance requirements can be met	
MARITAL STATUS	whether the applicant is single, married, divorced, engaged, separated, widowed, or living common-law	if transfer or travel is part of the job, the applicant can be asked if he or she can meet these requirements	
	whether an applicant's spouse is subject to transfer	ask whether there are any circumstances that might prevent completion of a minimum service commitment	information on dependants can be determined after selection if necessary
	about spouse's employment		
FAMILY STATUS	number of children or dependants	if the applicant would be able to work the required hours and, where applicable, overtime	contacts for emergencies and/or details on dependents can be determined after selection
	about child care arrangements		
NATIONAL OR ETHNIC ORIGIN	about birth-place, nationality of ancestors, spouse, or other relatives	since those who are entitled to work in Canada must be citizens, permanent residents, or holders of valid work permits, applicants can be asked if they are legally entitled to work in Canada	documentation of eligibility to work (papers, visas, etc.) can be requested after selection
	whether born in Canada		
	for proof of citizenship		

A GUIDE TO
SCREENING AND SELECTION IN EMPLOYMENT

SUBJECT	AVOID ASKING	PREFERRED	COMMENT
MILITARY SERVICE	about military service in other countries	inquiry about Canadian military service where employment preference is given to veterans by law	
LANGUAGE	mother tongue where language skills obtained	ask if applicant understands, reads, writes, or speaks languages required for the job	testing or scoring applicants for language proficiency is not permitted unless job-related
RACE OR COLOUR	any inquiry into race or colour, including colour of eyes, skin, or hair		
PHOTOGRAPHS	for photo to be attached to applications or sent to interviewer before interview		photos for security passes or company files can be taken after selection
RELIGION	about religious affiliation, church membership, frequency of church attendance		
	if applicant will work a specific religious holiday	explain the required work shift, asking if such a schedule poses problems for the applicant	reasonable accommodation of an employee's religious beliefs is the employer's duty
	for references from clergy or religious leader		
HEIGHT & WEIGHT			no inquiry unless there is evidence they are genuine occupational requirements
DISABILITY	for listing of all disabilities, limitations or health problems	ask if applicant has any condition that could affect ability to do the job	a disability is only relevant to job ability if it:

A GUIDE TO
SCREENING AND SELECTION IN EMPLOYMENT

SUBJECT	AVOID ASKING	PREFERRED	COMMENT
DISABILITY (Cont'd)	whether applicant drinks or uses drugs whether applicant has ever received psychiatric care or been hospitalized for emotional problems whether aplicant has received worker's compensation	ask if the applicant has any condition which should be considered in selection	- threatens the safety or property of others - prevents the applicant from safe and adequate job performance even when reasonable efforts are made to accommodate the disability
MEDICAL INFORMATION	if currently under physician's care name of family doctor		medical exams should be conducted after selection and only if an employee's condition is related to job duties
	if receiving counselling or therapy		Offers of employment can be made conditional on successful completion of a medical
PARDONED CONVICTION	whether an applicant has ever been convicted if an applicant has ever been arrested whether an applicant has a criminal record	if bonding is a job requirement ask if applicant is eligible	inquiries about criminal record/convictions are discouraged unless related to job duties
SEXUAL ORIENTATION	any inquiry about the applicant's sexual orientation		contacts for emergencies and/or details on dependents can be determined after selection
REFERENCES			the same restrictions that apply to questions asked of applicants apply when asking for employment references

A GUIDE TO
SCREENING AND SELECTION IN EMPLOYMENT

SUBJECT	AVOID ASKING	PREFERRED	COMMENT
MAKING INTERVIEW NOTES			Usually, interviewers will have copies of résumés or applications available at the interview for easy reference or to use as the basis of interview questions. When many applicants are being interviewed, interviewers often make notes on the résumés to help differentiate candidates. Even though these notes may be solely for the use of the interviewer, they must not identify or differentiate candidates according to prohibited grounds (for example, "black woman, 45ish" or "South Asian man").

Reproduced with permission of the Minister of Public Works and Government Services, 1995.

The request for irrelevant personal information can cause serious problems later if an employee is not given the job. A prospective employee can claim that he or she was denied the job because of the information he or she divulged, on request, at the interview. While this may only be the employee's perception, it can be enough to cast doubt on the selection process. In fact, even if the ultimate decision was primarily based on objective reasons, the interviewing employer can be found guilty of discrimination. This can happen if the irrelevant information influenced the employer's decision at all. If you don't need to know the information to help you fill the job requirements of the position, don't ask. No one can be blamed then for making the decision about the job based on any irrelevant personal information obtained.

EMPLOYEES

Co-workers

One of the most common sources of harassment in the workplace is an employee's co-workers. Typically, employees spend many hours everyday with their fellow employees so this is hardly surprising. Co-workers have the most contact with each other and consequently the greatest number of opportunities to harass each other. Some behaviour would lend itself more readily to co-worker harassment, such as:

- racist or sexist jokes;
- demeaning comments or taunting;
- comments or questions about one's "love life";
- offensive visual displays, such as posters and calendars.

Each of these behaviours could occur in the interaction between employees. Where employees are in similar positions or in any type of relationship in which there is not a power element, presumably one employee could simply advise another employee that the conduct was not welcome. This possibility is increased when the employees work in an atmosphere that has encouraged and supported the discussion of harassment issues, or indeed any issues of respect for their fellow workers.

The existence of either of the following conditions effectively prevents one employee from advising another that that conduct is offensive:

- a power element — if the harassing employee somehow holds a position of power over the other, whether it is real (for example, it can be seen on an organizational chart) or simply apparent to the harassed employee (for example, a dominant position in the pecking order at the job site or a dominant personality);
- a "closed" work environment — where open discussion is discouraged and employees do not want to be seen to rock the boat in any way.

Each of these scenarios can have an immediate negative effect on the resolution of harassment complaints.

The goal at each workplace is two-fold: to prevent harassment and also, as a back-up, to have in place an effective process for speedy resolution of any complaints should they arise. A critical element of this two-fold goal is to enable employees to speak up if they feel uncomfortable or offended. Harassment complaints can be avoided entirely if employees can simply state to the offending party that their comments or jokes are unwelcome. The most likely scenario in which this would happen is in worker-to-worker situations. If an employee does not feel sufficiently comfortable in this relationship or in the work environment as a whole to say "enough — stop already!" it is unlikely that he or she would feel able to do so with a supervisor, manager, boss or client.

Also, employees who feel unable to communicate their discomfort may let the situation simmer until it becomes completely intolerable. These situations can then result in complaints to the human rights commission, a hearing and ultimately a possible finding of liability against the employer who should have intervened (although note that under s. 45 of the Ontario *Human Rights Code*, employers can argue that they are not responsible for all co-worker harassment). If the employee can speak up sooner a potentially messy situation can be avoided and the employee's personal situation improved.

Co-workers have the greatest opportunity for harassment simply by virtue of their daily interaction. At the same time, they should be in the best position to put a stop to offending behaviour by fellow workers.

Supervisors and Managers

Another all-too-frequent source of harassment in the workplace is the employee's supervisors and managers. Harassment from this source can be more difficult to address from the employee's perspective because of the real or perceived power the supervisor/manager has over the employee. This can result in two scenarios that may be pictured by a concerned employee:

1. Reluctance to speak up. Employees may be hesitant to ask a supervisor or manager to stop making racist jokes, pinning up offensive cartoons or making sexual remarks or advances. The relative positions of the parties can make such a discussion awkward at best and frightening at worst.
2. Fear of retribution. Employees may be concerned that a complaint to another party regarding the actions or comments of a superior could affect their own jobs.

It is important to address these concerns in the development of a workplace harassment policy. One of the basic elements of any workplace harassment policy is that retribution against an employee who has spoken out will not be tolerated.

In addition, the policy must be adopted in conjunction with a training and awareness program to educate and sensitize all employees to issues of workplace harassment. Particular emphasis must be given to front-line supervisors and managers regarding the critical role they play in the process. The role of the supervisor and manager is discussed more fully in Chapters Five and Six.

Customers and Clients

Employees, of course, are protected from harassment they may encounter in the workplace. This includes harassment from co-workers, supervisors and managers, the most common sources of harassment. What is perhaps surprising is that employees may also be protected from harassment from any other third party with whom they come into contact in the course of their work. For example, employees can be protected from harassment that occurs in the workplace from suppliers and employees of other organizations such as couriers, repairers, technicians and caterers.

Finally, perhaps of greatest concern of all for many organizations, employers are responsible for ensuring that their workplace is free of harassment from *customers or clients*. Harassment is one area where the maxim "the customer is always right" is not accurate. Employees are not required to put up with harassment from a client or any other third party with whom they come into contact in the course of their employment. Of course, employees are expected to act reasonably if a customer or any other party makes inappropriate comments. The bottom line however is that the employer has control over the work environment and, as a result, is responsible for making it harassment-free and for responding to any complaints appropriately.

In one case, a hairdresser was racially harassed and then fired because of a substandard performance review. The tribunal highlighted the responsibility of the employer when third parties harass:

> It is clear, therefore, that when a complaint of harassment is received by an employer, whether the harassment is alleged to have originated from an employee or a third party, the employer is obliged to respond promptly and effectively with a thorough investigation, as well as with consideration for and sensitivity to the needs of the victim. (*Toth v. Sassy Cuts Inc.* (1987), 8 C.H.R.R. D/4376 (B.C. Human Rights Council))

One very difficult case involved an employee who assessed prison inmates, developed and recommended programs for them and reported on their suitability for release from the institution. The employee was subjected to abuse and assault in the course of his work. The tribunal hearing his complaint of racial harassment commented on the difficulties faced by an employer dealing with harassment by third parties:

> The Tribunal accepts that an employer is not required to maintain a pristine work environment, and that some work environments may be more difficult to manage than others. The Tribunal further accepts that threats from inmates are an unfortunate part of employment in the corrections system. However, the fact that such threats are not uncommon does not relieve the employer from its obligations under the law, although they may have some bearing on the assessment of the reasonableness and sufficiency of the respondent's response. (*Uzoaba v. Correctional Services of Canada* (1994), 94 C.L.L.C. 17,021 (Cdn. Human Rights Trib.), at page 60)

Finally, in one case in which a retail sales clerk ultimately lost her composure and swore back at a client who had called her "a f— Hindu who should never have been hired to work in a public-related service", the Council Member said:

> While an employer may not be able to control the remarks of a customer, or for that matter a co-worker or supervisor in the workplace, an employer does have control over how it responds to discriminatory conduct in that workplace, regardless of how the conduct occurred. It seems to me that the "unwelcome conduct" should not be treated any differently because that conduct was perpetrated by a customer. (*Mohammad v. Mariposa Stores Ltd.* (1991), 14 C.H.R.R. D/215 (B.C. Human Rights Council) at page D/218)

Employees are entitled to protection from harassment in the workplace regardless of the origin of the harassment. This means that employers must act to establish a harassment-free workplace through the use of policy, training, information and enforcement. However, if a third party, including a client, harasses an employee, the employer is still required to deal with the behaviour.

The response of the employer is what is critical in these circumstances. Human rights tribunals will understand that an external third party could act in an inappropriate manner, but will not be at all sympathetic if an employer does not follow up on complaints about the inappropriate behaviour quickly and seriously.

CHAPTER THREE

Where are People Protected?

THE WORKPLACE

Employees are protected from harassment that occurs at the workplace. The use of the term "workplace" however can be misleading. It can include an office, a job site, a sales call at a client's firm or a supplier's warehouse. Harassment that occurs away from the workplace may also be a violation of the employee's rights if it occurs while the employee is performing job functions.

The physical space that normally makes up the workplace is not as important as the fact that the employee is performing his or her job functions. Employees can be protected wherever they are as long as they are acting within the scope of their employment duties.

BUSINESS TRIPS

Employees are protected from harassment while away from the office if they are performing job-related functions. This means that business trips can be included within the "protected zone". The key question is whether the harassment takes place while the employee is engaged in his or her job duties.

In some cases, however, it is difficult to determine if the employee was participating in job-related functions while away from the workplace.

In a leading case, a human rights tribunal decided that an employee's trip to a work-related conference was not part of her job functions. In *Cluff v. Canada (Department of Agriculture)* (1992), 20 C.H.R.R. D/61 (Cdn. Human Rights Trib.), Lesley Cluff was employed as an information officer with Agriculture Canada. Her daily work was producing radio programs. She was also involved in the Eastern Canada Farm Writers Association (ECFWA), an organization that hosted conferences for its members and other interested non-members. Cluff was chair of the 1986 conference and was allowed to work on the planning of the conference during work hours as long as this did not interfere with her regular duties. Her employer paid for her registration at the conference but assumed no other costs. It was customary for Agriculture Canada employees to attend the ECFWA conferences, but not mandatory.

The tribunal decided that Cluff was performing two distinct duties at the conference. First, she was a representative of Agriculture Canada while attending the sessions. Second, she was acting as chair of the conference itself, not as an employee, when she was attending and hosting the conference hospitality suite.

One of Cluff's co-workers, Michael Sage, also attended the conference hospitality suite. Sage attended the conference on his own and at his own cost. Cluff alleged that she was sexually harassed by Sage at the conference hospitality suite. She complained that both Sage and Agriculture Canada had engaged in workplace harassment.

The employer argued that the acts alleged did not occur "in the course of employment" or "in matters related to employment" and therefore, the employer was not responsible. The employer also argued that the tribunal had no jurisdiction to hear the complaint because it was not employment related.

The employer reasoned that because it had no control over the conference the harassment did not occur in an employment-related situation. The tribunal set out some important criteria for deciding if harassment took place in the course of employment:

> An employee is in the course of employment when, within the period covered by the employment, he or she is carrying out:
>
> (1) activities which he or she might normally or reasonably do or be specifically authorized to do while so employed;
> (2) activities which fairly and reasonably may be said to be incidental to the employment or logically and naturally connected with it;
> (3) activities in furtherance of duties he or she owes to his or her employer; or
> (4) activities in furtherance of duties owed to the employer where the latter is exercising or could exercise control over what the employee does. (at page D/67)

The tribunal continued:

> An employee is still in the course of employment when he or she is carrying out intentionally or unintentionally, authorized or unauthorized, with or without the approval of his or her employer, activities which are discriminatory under the (*Canadian Human Rights Act*) and are in some way related or associated with the employment. However, an employee is considered to have deviated from the course of his or her employment when engaged in those activities which are not related to his or her employment or are personal in nature. (at page D/67)

In this case, the tribunal found that the employee's activities were not related to or associated with her employment. The employer did not require Cluff to work for or belong to the ECFWA. The tribunal decided that it was Cluff's own choice to belong to the organization, her employer had no control or authority over the conference, and her activities were of a personal nature. Consequently, the alleged harassment did not take place "in the course of employment" and/or "in matters related to employment".

Ultimately, the tribunal found that the *Canadian Human Rights Act* had not been violated because Cluff was not acting within the scope of her employment duties and that it had no jurisdiction to hear the complaint.

This case shows that the actions that might be work-related, and the areas that may make up the workplace, are perhaps best described as "fluid". The outcome in a similar case could be different if it could be shown that the connection between the employee and the harasser was different, or that the harasser was attending the conference as a representative of the employer or that organizing the hospitality suite was part of the employee's employment duties.

OFFICE PARTIES

Office parties can be difficult to categorize. Certainly, at first glance, it might appear that office parties would be outside the regular course of employment. However, there could be occasions at which employee participation is effectively mandatory and could perhaps be characterized as part of one's job duties.

Look again at the criteria established by the *Cluff* case, discussed immediately above, which determined whether participation at a work-related conference meant that the employee was acting within the scope of her employment duties.

The criteria for deciding whether an employee is acting within the scope of employment are whether the employee is carrying out:

(1) activities which he or she might normally or reasonably do or be specifically authorized to do while employed;
(2) activities which fairly and reasonably are incidental to the employment or are logically and naturally connected with it;
(3) activities in furtherance of duties he or she owes to his or her employer; or
(4) activities in furtherance of duties owed to the employer where the employer is exercising or could exercise control over what the employee does.

These are the criteria for deciding whether the employee is acting within the scope of employment duties. If so, any inappropriate behaviour directed at the employee may be harassment even if at first glance the activities he or she engages in appear to be social, such as at an office party or any other office function.

If the employee is acting in the course of employment, then the harassment is workplace harassment regardless of where or when it takes place. If the employee is engaging in activities of a personal nature, then the conduct is not workplace harassment.

This is not to say, however, that any conduct will be acceptable. If a co-worker, manager or supervisor engages in inappropriate, unwanted behaviour with another employee, it is a problem. Just because the conduct does not occur at work or during the course of an employee's duties, does not mean that it is acceptable behaviour. It simply means that it is not workplace harassment in the legal sense. The reality however is that the consequences of the behaviour may ultimately spill over to the workplace. The employee on the receiving end of the conduct will still be unhappy about it regardless of the label that is attached to it. This type of conduct may not be dealt with through the formal harassment process but if an employee is clearly unhappy because of a co-worker's actions, it should still be addressed. Regardless of where an incident occurred, it may ultimately impact the workplace.

AFTER-HOURS SOCIAL ACTIVITIES

Generally, after-hours social activities are not included as part of the workplace no matter how broad the definition. These activities include company-sponsored sports teams, the inter-office bowling league or an impromptu get-together for drinks after work. These are activities that are "personal in nature".

However, work-related activities may only have the appearance of a social activity. For example, taking a client out for dinner or to a hockey game or symphony where the employee is present only as a representative of the employer, may bring the activity within the meaning of employment duties.

Again, the test set out above in the *Cluff* case is helpful. The criteria in *Cluff* can pinpoint whether the employee was acting within the scope of his or her employment duties. If the employee was acting within the scope of employment duties, then unwelcome behaviour that has a negative impact on the workplace or the employee's ability to perform work duties can be harassment. These criteria include:

(1) activities that an employee normally or reasonably does, or that the employee might be authorized to do at work;
(2) activities that are part of the job;
(3) activities to help the employee perform their job; or
(4) activities to help the employee perform his or her job where the employer has control over what the employee does, whether or not the employer exercises that control.

Ultimately, the question is whether the employer had control over the activities or whether the activities were of a personal nature.

Generally, after-hours activities that involve a group of employees socializing are not within the scope of employment duties. However, any inappropriate behaviour that occurs at these functions has a "spill over" effect. That is, even if the behaviour does not fit the definition of harassment, the bottom line is that it is wrong and it was committed by a fellow worker. It is difficult to separate the behaviour, whether illegal or not, from the daily interaction of the employees. It would be surprising if the behaviour did not have an effect on the employee's relations at work, regardless of whether it is actually "harassment". This kind of situation still has to be resolved and cannot be ignored.

CHAPTER FOUR
Is this Harassment?

TYPICAL EXAMPLES

There are some typical and some not-so-typical examples of the kinds of behaviour that can constitute harassment. Also, perhaps just as importantly, there are examples of behaviour that are *not* harassment. Some of these examples are outlined below. Remember, however, that much of the conduct that may be harassment is in a grey area. Because harassment can be determined to a large part by the party on the receiving end, it is difficult to state with certainty in all cases that the behaviour will be harassment. Remember how important context is and when in doubt, the simplest and safest advice to offer an employee is — *don't* do it. There will always be another opportunity to tell a joke, make a comment or send an e-mail — either in the employee's own time away from the workplace or to the employee's friends away from work, rather than in front of a more "captive" audience of co-workers.

These examples are taken from the brochure, "Preventing Harassment", prepared by the Saskatchewan Women's Secretariat:

TEST YOUR KNOWLEDGE: IS THIS HARASSMENT?

1. *A regular customer often tells racist jokes even though staff have objected.*

   Jokes which demean or offend are considered a form of harassment.

2. *An employee constantly pressures a co-worker for a date, even though she has said she is not interested.*

   The persistent attention is unwanted and unwelcome, and therefore can constitute sexual harassment.

3. *Despite his interest, one employee who uses a wheelchair is not invited to participate in staff sports activities.*

   Excluding someone because of a disability can be a form of harassment.

4. *An employee often compliments a co-worker on her appearance. She likes the attention and often flirts back.*

   No, this is not sexual harassment. This is an example of a mutual relationship. It appears that both parties welcome the behaviour.

5. *A supervisor often uses racial stereotypes when referring to Aboriginal employees.*

   Making derogatory comments about a racial group can constitute harassment.

6. *A staff member is often ridiculed about his weight.*

   Derogatory comments or jokes about someone's physical size or weight can constitute harassment.

7. *After an employee turns down her supervisor's invitation for drinks, he cuts back her hours.*

   This could be a classic case of sexual harassment, if the boss uses his position of power to penalize an employee for not accepting his invitation.

Reprinted by permission of the Saskatchewan Women's Secretariat.

The Community Legal Information Association of P.E.I. Inc. has also published a broad description of behaviour that can constitute sexual harassment. The categories and examples are restricted to sexual harassment but indicate the breadth of types of behaviour that may be considered harassment. Here is an excerpt (please see Chapter Ten for the full version):

There are two categories of sexual harassment:

- inappropriate sexual requirements from your supervisor or employer;
- a destructive work environment where the conditions of employment include unwanted sexual advances, unwanted requests for sexual favours, and other unwanted verbal, written or physical behaviour of a sexual nature.

Some examples of harassment are:

- questions and discussions about sexual activities, suggestive remarks and innuendos, bragging about sexual prowess, and proposals of physical intimacy;
- being judged on physical attributes rather than skills;
- display of pornographic or sexually degrading material;
- practical jokes of a sexual nature which cause awkwardness or embarrassment;
- letters and notes expressing sexual intentions;
- leering or other gestures;
- unnecessary physical contact.

Sexual harassment is not sexual joking, flirtation and discussions of a sexual nature between two or more **EQUALLY CONSENTING** adults.

FLIRTATION AND DATING

A fine line exists between behaviour that might be considered harassment and behaviour that is welcome and social. This line becomes even finer when a romantic attraction exists between co-workers, or in an even more difficult although common situation, between a supervisor or manager and an employee.

One employer, B.C. Hydro, has included questions and answers regarding flirtation and dating (these are fully cited in Chapter Eight) in its information booklet about workplace harassment. These questions capture the concerns of many employees about harassment:

What if I only touched someone once and I didn't intend to offend? Will I be guilty of sexual harassment?

No, if it isn't repeated and the impact is minor. More than anything, people who are harassed want the behaviour to stop. If you didn't intend to offend, apologize and be willing to change your behaviour. The key is not to do it again.

However, a single incident can be considered sexual harassment if it has significant impact on the person. Under the human rights law, lack of intent to harass is not considered a defense. The courts are not interested in what a harasser "intended". They are concerned with the impact of the action on the person who has been harassed.

The key is to be responsible. Be aware of the potential affect of your actions on others.

Are friendly touching and "horsing around" okay?

Some people enjoy non-sexual touching. But if touch is not welcome then it isn't appropriate or friendly. Some people dislike all forms of physical contact and others feel pressured or offended by touching from someone who has authority over them. Still others welcome a friendly hug at an appropriate time.

Remember too that some cultures have different customs regarding touch. For example, while a handshake or hug may be considered an appropriate greeting in some cultures, in others these actions may be taken as offensive.

And even more to the point, the following two questions are included in the booklet:

Can I ask someone for a date?

Some people may welcome an invitation to socialize. But pressuring someone for a date after they've clearly refused is not acceptable.

Is it okay to become romantically involved with a co-worker?

An individual's personal life is not the employer's concern and job decisions must be based solely on work-related performances and abilities. To do anything else is discrimination. However, there is a possibility of conflict of interest, particularly when a relationship exists between a supervisor and a co-worker. In this situation, regardless of how impartial all business judgements are, there may be the suspicion of special favours.

Some important cases have dealt with sexual harassment and sexual relationships between co-workers. The cases have emphasized that the protection of employees' human rights does not amount to a total ban on social or sexual relationships between colleagues. In the first case to deal with sexual harassment, *Bell v. Ladas* (1980), 1 C.H.R.R. D/155 (Ont. Bd. of Inquiry), the adjudicator said that it was important to separate the ban on harassing behaviour from normal social interaction between employees:

> The prohibition of such conduct is not without its dangers. One must be cautious that the law not inhibit normal social contact between management and employees or normal discussion between management and employees. It is not abnormal, nor should it be prohibited activity for a supervisor to become socially involved with an employee. *An invitation to dinner is not an invitation to a complaint.* (at page D/156, original emphasis)

The adjudicator in that case said that it would be a problem if the social relationship was felt to be a required part of the job:

> *The danger or the evil that is to be avoided is* **coerced** *or* **compelled** *social contact where the employee's refusal to participate may result in a loss of employment benefits.* Such coercion or compulsion may be overt or subtle but if any feature of employment becomes reasonably dependent on reciprocating a social relationship proffered by a member of management, then the overture becomes a condition of employment and may be considered to be discriminatory. (at page D/156, original emphasis)

So, if an employee feels that he or she has to participate in the relationship or that the relationship is a condition of employment, then the actions become harassment. This use or abuse of power would typically have to occur between an employee and a manager or supervisor. An employee of equal status or power would probably find it difficult to make another employee feel that a relationship was a condition of employment when they had no ability to hire, fire or promote. However, in some instances, an employee could still create a negative impact in the workplace for his or her co-worker by simply making his or her life miserable. This is simply the exercise of another form of power that might not be reflected in any organizational chart but is still felt. This could particularly be the case when the coercion takes place with the tacit approval of management, or their acquiescence.

In another important case, *Dupuis v. British Columbia (Ministry of Forests)* (1993), 20 C.H.R.R. D/87 (B.C. Human Rights Council), a supervisor and a student/employee began a sexual relationship. This case is a good example of how difficult it may be for a manager to tell if his or her own behaviour is harassment.

Linda Dupuis was a graduate student in Zoology at the University of British Columbia and a researcher with the Ministry of Forests, Forest Sciences Division of the British Columbia government. She was employed to coordinate a survey project of forest birds in the Queen Charlotte Islands. She reported to two supervisors, one of whom was Dave Seip, a wildlife biologist with the Ministry of Forests as well as an adjunct professor at UBC.

Seip drove Dupuis to the Queen Charlotte Islands to begin her survey work. The first day they drove for about six hours, stopping for the night in Williams Lake. When they stopped, Dupuis waited in the truck while Seip made arrangements for the night. They did not discuss the arrangements. Seip rented one room with two beds. Dupuis did not voice any objections to this arrangement.

After dinner and a walk they returned to their room where Dupuis began to read. Seip had a shower and began to watch television sitting on his bed. Dupuis moved to Seip's bed so that she could watch the news on television without her contact lenses. Shortly after that, Seip kissed and embraced Dupuis. After some time she asked him to stop, which he did. They remained on his bed where they fell asleep. Prior to falling asleep, he asked her if she found him attractive; she said "yes". Sometime during the night he began to caress her again, and at that time they had sexual intercourse. This sexual relationship continued for approximately one week.

Seip remained in the Queen Charlottes for approximately three weeks. While he was there the working relationship between him and Dupuis was unpleasant. She sometimes yelled at him and was often in tears. After Seip left, Dupuis spoke to him by telephone on several occasions. He told her that he would be able to get her funding for her Master's thesis. She subsequently contacted another professor and informed him that she did not want Seip involved with her thesis. On Dupuis' return to Vancouver, she filed a complaint of sexual harassment.

The critical issue in this case was whether Dupuis welcomed the sexual contact. Did she participate in a consensual sexual relationship with her supervisor? The Member Designate who ultimately heard this case at the British Columbia Human Rights Council decided that the relationship was not consensual. The Member began by recognizing that "(h)uman rights legislation does not prohibit social or sexual contact between management and employees" (at page D/92).

After stating that social and sexual relationships are not necessarily harassment, the Member addressed the issues that arise because of the power that managers can have over employees:

> However, because of the imbalance of power that often exists between managers and their employees, *managers must be very careful to insure that they are not taking advantage of their position of authority* to import sexual requirements into the job. In my view, the burden rests with the manager to be certain that any sexual contact is welcomed by the employee and continues to be welcomed. (at page D/92)

The Member acknowledged that in this case, the employee had voluntarily participated in a sexual relationship with her supervisor. However, he said that the fact that Dupuis voluntarily engaged in sexual intercourse was not the deciding factor of the question "was the conduct welcome?" At page D/93, the Member cited a United States Supreme Court case, *Meritor Savings Bank v. Vincent*, 106 S. Ct. 2399, 40 E.P.D. 36,159 (1986), where an employee alleged that she submitted to sexual intercourse to avoid jeopardizing her employment:

> [T]he fact that sex-related conduct was "voluntary", in the sense that the complainant was not forced to participate against her will, is not a defense to a sexual harassment suit .... The gravamen of any sexual harassment claim is that the alleged sexual advances were "unwelcome" . . . While the question whether particular conduct was indeed unwelcome presents difficult problems of proof and turns largely on credibility determinations committed to the trier of fact, the District Court in this case erroneously focused on the "voluntariness" of respondent's participation in the claimed sexual episodes. The correct inquiry is whether the respondent by her conduct indicated that the alleged sexual advances were unwelcome, not whether her actual participation in sexual intercourse was voluntary.

The Member agreed that acquiescence or participation in the sexual activity was not the determining question. Rather, the critical issue was still *whether the conduct was welcome*.

An assessment of whether sexual activity is welcome turns on two criteria: first, the complainant's behaviour and second, whether the alleged harasser knew or ought to have known that his conduct was unwelcome. Regarding the first point, the Member asked whether Dupuis' behaviour was consistent with the allegation that the sexual activity was unwelcome. There was evidence to indicate that she welcomed the conduct, including joining Seip on his bed to watch television, returning his initial physical advances, telling him that she was attracted to him. But, there was also strong evidence that she did not welcome the sexual conduct. Dupuis told Seip she did not want to have sex, she did not want co-workers to know of their involvement, and her behaviour at the job site was consistent with her position. Taken together, the Member decided that Dupuis did not welcome the conduct.

The Member also found, however, that Seip believed that the sexual activity was welcome. The Member cautioned that Seip's belief was not a deciding factor of the issue of welcomeness. The Member said:

> People vary in their ability to recognize the non-verbal signals given by those around them. Some are sensitive to subtle nuances of voice tone and body language, others are oblivious to all but the most explicit expressions. Further, even though capable of recognizing signs of objection, a person may be blinded by his purpose. While the perception of the alleged harasser is relevant in determining whether the conduct was unwelcome, the proper question to ask is whether a reasonable person would recognize that the conduct in those circumstances was unwelcome. What is reasonable will depend on all the circumstances, including the nature of the impugned conduct and the relationship. (at page D/95)

This case is an excellent example of the difficulties involved in entering into sexual relationships with co-workers, and particularly with employees in a reporting relationship. Even if a manager believes that a relationship is consensual, it may be harassment. By the same token, even if an employee is participating in a sexual relationship with another employee or a manager, the relationship can still be harassment. The critical issue is whether the activity is welcome. The test for welcomeness is not whether the employee participates in a relationship, but the behaviour of the employee and whether the manager knew or ought to have known that the behaviour was unwelcome.

JOKES AND COMMENTS

Jokes and comments are probably the most common area of harassment on a day-to-day basis at the workplace. They are also probably the area in which the most improvement can be made. This is because often the employee making the comment or repeating the joke is not aware that he or she is making another employee feel insulted or degraded. If the offending employee is approached in the right way, there can be an opportunity to counteract the harassment before people take positions that make it difficult to settle the matter quickly and informally. See Chapter Six, What Can Be Done About It?, for more information on the steps that employers and employees can take.

A good starting point is recognizing the power of words to hurt an individual. The power of language cannot be overestimated. While most individuals would, if they stopped to consider it, be aware of the inappropriateness of a joke, comment or name, the effect of many other comments is more subtle. The impact of both the written and the spoken word is immeasurable. What can appear to be a minor, even negligible issue to some can be the substance of a terrible insult to another.

Language can exclude or include groups that might be marginalized. A simple term can become an unintended, but powerful, message. For example, the use of gender-neutral language might appear to be a pointless exercise in political correctness for some and a strong act of inclusion for others. In some cases, the insistence of the use of outmoded terms to describe different workplace activities, jobs or positions can be seen as a type of gender harassment.

The following terms demonstrate the use of language that could be gender harassment if used frequently. The list also includes some of the recommended alternatives. Often the alternative provides a far better description of the actual activity or job. And often the continued use of the original term may convey an attitude that the individual who is being referred to is not on an equal footing. For example, the use of the phrase "lady lawyer" rather than simply, lawyer, somehow denotes that the lawyer in question is somehow different from other "regular" lawyers.

Gender-based	Neutral
Businessman, businessmen	Business person, executive
Cameraman	Camera operator
Chairman	Chairperson
Policeman	Police officer
Fireman	Firefighter
Airline stewardess	Flight attendant
Manpower	Human resources, work force
Man-made	Synthetic, artificial
To man (verb)	To staff
Workmen's compensation	Workers' compensation

When in doubt, ask an individual, don't assume, how he or she prefers to be addressed. Then use that term, not another.

Another way in which language can be a harassment problem is when the discussion centres on sexual practices, activities or preferences. This type of "locker room" talk often forms the basis of sexual harassment complaints. Many employees find it unwelcome and offensive.

The spectre of workplace harassment is not however supposed to result in the equivalent of a gag order in the workplace. Just because some comments can be harassment does not mean that employees should end up with the feeling that they should say nothing, rather than risk a harassment complaint. There are still many areas that can be discussed in the workplace. Even so-called danger areas, like sex, can be alright. In an important early case on sexual harassment, *Bell v. Ladas* (1980), 1 C.H.R.R. D/155 (Ont. Bd. of Inquiry), the adjudicator said:

Again, The Code ought not to be seen or perceived as inhibiting free speech. If sex cannot be discussed between supervisor and employee neither can other values such as race, colour or creed, which are contained in The Code, be discussed. Thus, differences of opinion by an employee where sexual matters are discussed may not involve a violation of The Code; it is only when the language or words may be reasonably construed to form a condition of employment that the Code provides a remedy. Thus, the frequent and persistent taunting by a supervisor of an employee because of his or her colour is discriminatory under The Code and, similarly, the frequent and persistent taunting of an employee by a supervisor because of his or her sex is discriminatory activity under The Code. (at page D/156)

POSTERS, CALENDARS AND PICTURES

"What about the pin-up calendars that our best supplier gives the guys? We'd be snubbing the supplier if we didn't show our appreciation by hanging them up. What about the firefighter calendars? The women all have those, and now you're telling us that we can't have one small pin-up?"

This can often be the discussion that follows the introduction of a "no poster" rule. These rules are implemented because visual images can also be harassment. Usually this is the case in sexual harassment, but it also occurs with respect to racial harassment.

Today, inappropriate visual images can include not only posters and calendars but also computer screen savers, e-mail messages and cartoons.

Rather than a blanket "no posters" rule, workplaces should consider the introduction of a "no inappropriate posters" rule. This gives employees some discretion to decide if they feel their own posters and calendars might be a problem. If they have any questions they should approach one of the individuals identified in the harassment policy to ask for a second opinion. However, the fact that something is questionable is often a good enough indication that it could be over the line. These are the posters and calendars that might be best appreciated for their artistic qualities in the privacy of the employee's own home. Of course, if they would not be welcome at home, then the employee has a very clear indication that the poster or calendar is offensive.

CHAPTER FIVE
Who is Responsible? What are the Consequences?

HARASSER-EMPLOYEE TERMINATION AND WRONGFUL DISMISSAL

Harassers are, of course, responsible for their own actions. Following an investigation, typically done by the employer or an outside third party, an employer will make a decision about whether the harassment took place and what happened. (See Chapter Nine, How to Investigate?) If the employer — or in some union environments, a joint committee or even an arbitration board — decides that the behaviour did take place and that it was harassment, the individuals who caused the harassment may be disciplined up to the point of termination of employment.

The workplace harassment policy should outline the range of disciplinary options that could be enforced if an employee harasses another employee. The policy should clearly state that employees can be disciplined for engaging in harassment and that the discipline potentially includes termination of employment.

Some caution should be interjected at this point, however. A zero tolerance policy mandating instant dismissal for employees who harass other employees is not appropriate. The focus of human rights law is not to punish offenders. Human rights law focuses instead on a remedy for the victim and on stopping the discriminatory behaviour. This principle should be kept in mind in employee disciplinary proceedings.

Once there has been a finding of harassment and an appropriate remedy has been decided, attention must turn to the harasser. The human rights context should not be abandoned once the findings are made; neither should the employment law context. Some employees who are fired for harassing co-workers will sue their employer for wrongful dismissal. A surprising number of these cases are won by the employee. Surprising because they are decided after the employer has conducted investigations and thorough reviews of the rights of the harassed employee and their own responsibility to enforce their harassment policy.

In one such case, *Wright v. British Columbia Trade and Development Corp.* (1994), 3 C.C.E.L. (2d) 254 (B.C.S.C.), an employee was fired because he was involved in a prank sending g-string panties in the inter-office mail to a female corporate vice-president, among others, and signed another male senior employee's name. The employee initially denied his involvement in the activity, but later admitted he had taken part along with some co-workers.

The court reviewed the situation and decided that the employee had been wrongfully dismissed. It awarded the employee damages in lieu of notice of his dismissal. The court said:

> There is not here a revelation of character which indicates dishonesty or untrustworthiness or a deliberate disobedience of corporate direction. There was no justification for coming to the conclusion that this employee was unfit for a position of trust and confidence or that his conduct was incompatible with the due and faithful discharge of his duty. Accordingly, the plaintiff is entitled to damages.

In another case, *Bannister v. General Motors of Canada Ltd.* (1994), 8 C.C.E.L. (2d) 281 (Ont. Gen. Div.), an employee was found by the employer to have harassed several female employees. In spite of the fact that the employer had a written policy in place prohibiting harassment and had provided training to its employees about harassment, the court found that the dismissal was unwarranted. The court said that the employer had not stated in the policy or in the training that employees could actually be fired for harassment.

SUPERVISORS AND MANAGERS

Supervisors and managers play a critical role in two important respects. First, because of their front-line position, supervisors and front-line managers can do more than any other employee group to be aware of harassment and to protect employees from it. Second, they are the most likely individuals to be enforcing the policy on a day-to-day basis, setting the tone and following up on any potential harassment.

Supervisors and managers have been front and centre in several cases on harassment. In one case, an employee who was mentally disabled quit his employment after he could no longer endure the behaviour of his supervisor. The board said:

> The crux of the harassment in the instant case is the humiliation the complainant received from his supervisor. He was treated as inferior, as someone who did not deserve the same respect as the so-called normal

employee. Although the name-calling was not all that frequent, the pervasive environment for Mr. Boehm in his relationship with Mr. Woods was one of disrespect, because Mr. Woods regarded Mr. Boehm as inferior because of this handicap, and let him know this.... *(Boehm v. National System of Baking Ltd.* (1987), 8 C.H.R.R. D/4110 (Ont. Bd. of Inquiry), at page D/4122)

Another case also acknowledged the importance of the actions of the supervisor or manager. The case went so far as to include situations in which the manager did not actively take part in the behaviour but simply allowed it to continue. The board said:

It is now beyond question that the atmosphere in which an employee must work is a condition of his or her employment, and should that atmosphere be oppressed or "poisoned" for a minority group, that circumstance might amount to discrimination on a prohibited basis. *Management personnel who know, or ought to know, of that condition but permit it to continue thereby discriminate against the affected employees even if they are not themselves actively engaged in the production of that atmosphere.* (*Ghosh v. Domglas Inc.* (1992), 17 C.H.R.R. D/216 (Ont. Bd. of Inquiry), at page D/227, emphasis added)

The role of the supervisor is important. He or she can help keep the workplace free from harassment. Alternatively, the supervisor can, through active participation or acquiescence, create an atmosphere of disrespect where harassment is tolerated.

Supervisors must be aware of the workplace harassment policy, the process that is to be followed, and the importance of their own role. An employer must provide training for this group even if resources are not available to train the entire staff. Individuals who fill these positions can make or break the harassment policy. (See Chapter Six, What Can Be Done About It?, for steps managers and supervisors can take.)

UNIONS

Unions can provide an effective way to address and combat harassment in the workplace. Many of them have worked hard to include non-discrimination clauses in their collective agreements. They have also been able to devote resources to help their members grieve discrimination when it occurs in the workplace. Many unions have also included demands for joint committees to deal with harassment in the workplace in their collective bargaining processes.

The Supreme Court of Canada decided in *Renaud v. Central Okanagan School District No. 23*, [1992] 2 S.C.R. 970, that unions may be jointly responsible with employers for discriminatory workplace conditions. The *Renaud* case addressed the union's duty to accommodate its members when the members encounter discrimination. This responsibility may easily extend to making reasonable efforts to provide employees with harassment-free workplaces. Also, unions are in a good position to provide support for employees who have been harassed or who have concerns about harassment.

But unions have a potentially difficult role to play in representing employees involved in harassment. The most difficult issue arises in intra-union disputes. This can occur when both the harassed employee, who has grieved the harassment as a violation of the collective agreement, and the alleged harasser, who has requested some representation because the complaint could result in discipline, demand union representation. The potential for conflict of interest may overwhelm any attempt to ensure a fair hearing for all parties.

Unions have duties to both employees, just as employers would in a similar non-union situation. A union that refuses to represent an employee who is grieving the actions of another union member, or that provides only token representation to the grievor, is not fulfilling its role.

Unions are challenged in these circumstances to ensure that both parties' interests are safeguarded and advanced appropriately. This is no different, however, from the challenge facing employers in non-union workplaces who investigate and resolve harassment issues internally. They also have a duty to all their employees as the unions do to all their members.

COMPANIES

Employers can be responsible for the discriminatory acts of their employees where those actions are work-related. In *Robichaud v. Brennan*, [1987] 2 S.C.R. 84, 8 C.H.R.R. D/4326, the Supreme Court of Canada decided that the employer was in the best position to deal with harassment:

> Indeed, if the Act is concerned with the effects of discrimination rather than its cause (or motivations), it must be admitted that *only an employer can remedy undesirable effects; only an employer can provide the most important remedy — a healthy work environment.* (at page D/4333, emphasis added)

The court concluded that the human rights legislation requires that employers be held liable for the discriminatory acts of their employees where those actions are work-related.

Harassers are the individuals who actually make the pass, fondle the co-worker, tell the racist joke or use the inappropriate name. So why aren't they the ones who are sued or complained about? In truth, they often are, but not as often as the organization that employs them. In one important case dealing with this issue, the court provided this rationale for corporate liability:

The next issue to be decided is the extent of liability under the Code. If a foreman or supervisor discriminates because of sex, will the company be liable? The law is quite clear that companies are liable where members of management, no matter what the rank, engage in other forms of discriminatory activity. Thus, companies have been held liable where lower ranking members of the management team engage in anti-union activity or discriminate against employees because of race or colour, and the same general law that imposes liability in those cases ought to apply where members of the management team discriminate because of sex. Thus, I would have no hesitation in finding the corporate respondent liable for a violation of the Code if one of its officers engaged in prohibited conduct and, indeed, the same liability would attach if the violator had a lower rank on the management team. (*Bell v. Ladas* (1980), 1 C.H.R.R. D/155 (Ont. Bd. of Inquiry), at page D/156)

The most common example of workplace harassment takes place between co-workers or between a supervisor or a manager and an employee. This is also one of the primary reasons that employers are liable for the harassment of their employees. The courts have recognized that most incidents of harassment occur between employees and have identified employers as the party most able to influence the actions of their employees.

Employers have also been held responsible for the harassment of their employees by persons other than their fellow employees. The rationale is that employers are responsible for providing a workplace free of harassment for their employees. This can include harassment from clients, members of the public, suppliers, couriers, repairers or any individual with whom an employee may come into contact as part of the job. The employer is required in such a situation to take reasonable measures once informed of the harassment. (See *Janzen v. Platy Enterprises Ltd.*, [1989] 1 S.C.R. 1252, 10 C.H.R.R. D/6205.)

In *Broadfield v. De Havilland/Boeing of Canada Ltd.* (1993), 19 C.H.R.R. D/347 (Ont. Bd. of Inquiry), an employee who became the first female supervisor was harassed by the men with whom she worked. The employer argued that it was not responsible for the actions of those employees. The board however said that it was responsible if it failed to prevent or respond appropriately to the complaints:

> ... harassment by fellow employees because of gender will not make the company automatically liable. However, the company will be liable if its management personnel fail to take adequate steps to prevent the harassment and failed to take adequate steps to deal with the harassment once it occurred.

The board in that case also found that the employer had been aware of the potential for problems when asking Broadfield to act as the first female supervisor. In spite of this, the employer did not take any steps to prevent or mitigate any harassing behaviour. The board concluded:

The company did not effectively stand by Ms. Broadfield after putting her in a position where they knew she would experience difficulty. (at page D/368)

Burton v. Chalifour Bros. Construction Ltd. (1994), 21 C.H.R.R. D/501 (B.C. Human Rights Council), which was discussed in Chapter One, is a similar case involving gender harassment in the construction industry. A carpenter-lather had been employed in the construction business for 11 years and complained of sexual harassment by her co-workers. Her employer conceded that the conduct to which she had been subjected was harassment, but argued that its response to her complaints was sufficient to avoid an award being made against it.

The Council found that the employer had not taken appropriate steps to address Karen Burton's complaints. The Council Member stated:

...employers have a responsibility to maintain a workplace free of discrimination. An employer's failure to respond quickly and effectively to a complaint of harassment may increase the remedial consequences to the employer by perpetuating the discriminatory environment.

The Member cited a passage from an earlier case, *Kotyk v. Canadian Employment and Immigration Commission* (1983), 4 C.H.R.R. D/1416 (Cdn. Human Rights Trib.), which outlined the employer's responsibilities to maintain a workplace free from harassment:

What responsibility does an employer have to provide employees with a workplace free from the fear of sexual harassment? First, managers and supervisors must themselves be aware that sexual harassment is prohibited conduct under the Act. When a complaint is made, it must be dealt with a serious matter, not by a gentle tap on the fingers, but as a potential breach of a statute. Employers should advise their employees that sexual interplay that has, or may reasonably appear to have, employment consequences — either direct, in the nature of firing, loss of benefits, etc. or indirect, such as an adverse effect on the work environment — is improper. The distinction between flirtation and harassment should be clarified. Complaint mechanisms should be in place, so that complaints can be made confidentially and without fear of reprisals. Employers have a responsibility to advise their supervisory personnel and employees about the significance and consequences of sexual harassment. (at page D/1430)

The Member found that the employer was responsible for the harassment suffered by Burton. In addition, in a highly unusual step, it found Thomas Chalifour, the owner and sole director and officer of the employer company, to be jointly and severally liable with the company for the compensation awarded to the employee. It found support for this award in an earlier case, *Primack v. Azim Enterprises Co. Ltd.* (1991), 14 C.H.R.R. D/150 (B.C. Human Rights Council):

Since the employer's liability flows from its control over and responsibility to provide a work environment free of discrimination ... the manner in which a director, acting in a managerial capacity, responded to a request to redress a discriminatory situation might attract individual liability. (at page D/151)

Interestingly, but perhaps not surprisingly, the Member held Thomas Chalifour jointly liable even though he had testified that he had delegated responsibility for day-to-day operations to his company supervisors. The Member concluded:

This delegation of his managerial responsibilities to Company employees does not relieve him as the senior manager, of liability for management's inadequate response to Burton's complaints of harassment....

Both Thomas Chalifour and the company, Chalifour Bros. Construction Ltd., were ordered to compensate Burton a total of approximately $20,000.

In a case that dealt with racial harassment, *Hinds v. Canada (Employment and Immigration Comm.)* (1988), 10 C.H.R.R. D/5683, 24 C.C.E.L. 65 (Cdn. Human Rights Trib.), the board also reviewed the role of the employer with respect to harassment that occurs within its organization. Again, the board focused on the need to respond in an effective way to harassment:

Although the *(Canadian Human Rights Act)* does not impose a duty on an employer to maintain a pristine working environment, there is a duty upon an employer to take prompt and effectual action when it knows or should know of co-employees' conduct in the workplace amounting to racial harassment ... To satisfy the burden upon it, the employer's response should bear some relationship to the seriousness of the incident itself ... To avoid liability, the employer is obliged to take reasonable steps to alleviate, as best it can, the distress arising within the work environment and to reassure those concerned that it is committed to the maintenance of a workplace free of racial harassment.

Several provincial human rights commissions have published guidelines or other information regarding the position and responsibility of the employer with respect to harassment. Following are excerpts from these guidelines (they are fully reproduced in Chapter Ten).

The Alberta Human Rights Commission included the following warning in its publication on sexual harassment. The information contained in this publication would apply to other forms of discriminatory harassment as well.

Who is legally responsible?

The Supreme Court of Canada has decided that in cases of proven sexual harassment employers are responsible for the actions of their employees.

Lack of awareness by management does not necessarily eliminate this liability.

Employer responsibilities

In Alberta, employers are responsible for maintaining a work environment free from sexual harassment for all employees, customers and clients.

A supervisor who neglects to follow up on a complaint of sexual harassment may be liable under the *Individual's Rights Protection Act* for failing to take prompt and appropriate action.

Not having an effective policy on sexual harassment in place can increase an employer's liability in the event of a complaint being filed. Prompt and appropriate action on sexual harassment complaints can reduce employer liability still further.

In Manitoba, the Human Rights Commission set out in its Fact Sheet (of April 18, 1988) the consequences for employees and others who do not take action against harassment:

Why should you act?

Employers, landlords and service providers are legally obligated to take reasonable steps to provide an environment free from harassment. Failure to do so can result in:

- a poisoned business environment
- loss of productivity and business
- high rate of staff or tenant turnover
- a human rights complaint
- payment of monetary compensation if the complaint is substantiated
- damage to your reputation

In New Brunswick, the Human Rights Commission highlights in its publication a "carrot and stick" approach, stating both the negative and potentially positive cost-saving aspects of workplace harassment:

Are employers responsible for preventing sexual harassment?

Yes. An employer who has not taken appropriate steps to prevent sexual harassment is liable for harassment by managers and other employees, even if the employer was unaware of the harassment. In certain cases, employers may be also be liable when employees harass customers or are harassed by them. Accordingly, it is important for employers to develop policies and procedures on sexual harassment.

Why is it good business for employers to prevent sexual harassment?

Sexual harassment may result in stress, increased sick leave, low morale, low productivity and high turnover. Complaints of sexual harassment can also consume a great deal of time and lead to negative publicity and major legal expenses.

The Nova Scotia Human Rights Commission focuses on the reasons why an employer should *want* to prevent workplace harassment in its publication:

Statistics show that sexual harassment is a serious problem which affects society as a whole. Using the workplace as an example, consider the implications sexual harassment has for those involved.

- The employee being harassed may experience physical and mental health problems.
- On-the-job harassment means poor work performance and strained relations with other co-workers.
- The stress of experiencing sexual harassment has a personal effect on life after work hours as well.
- Relationships with family members and friends may suffer.
- Companies are also concerned about sexual harassment because sexual harassment complaints affect their reputations in the community, result in staff turnover, and productivity lessens.
- Even if a company has a sexual harassment policy in place, liability for the acts of its employee may still result.
- Although the workplace is used as an example, sexual harassment is prohibited in all areas of public life and this includes the provision of accommodation, services, and facilities.

Finally, the Newfoundland Human Rights Commission includes a brief reference to employers in its harassment publication that seems to downplay the responsibility of the employer:

As an employer:

Your responsibility

As an employer you should know that it you are aware of any civil misbehaviour of your employees, you may be held accountable. If one of your employees is successfully charged with sexual harassment against a person under his/her supervision, under the *Human Rights Code*, you as the employer can be made a party to that complaint.

It is well-accepted law that employers are responsible for protecting their employees from harassment to which they are subjected in the course of their employment. Employers are responsible for providing employees with workplaces that are free of harassment. If this does not occur, the employer can be liable for harassment that occurs within the course of employment for any of its employees. The only possible defence an employer may have is to demonstrate that it did everything possible to prevent the harassment, and that when the harassment did occur, the employer responded quickly, seriously and effectively.

CHAPTER SIX

What Can Be Done About It?

STEPS INDIVIDUALS CAN TAKE

Harassment occurs at an individual level. It is one employee or a group of individual employees who actively take part in, or who ignore, harassing behaviour. It is also felt on an individual level. The good news is that just as one person can cause harassment, one person can also do a lot to stop harassment.

The first step is to be able to identify harassing behaviour. One of the sample workplace harassment policies in Chapter Eight includes answers to some common questions about harassment. It was prepared by B.C. Hydro. The questions and answers in the policy focus on the personal responsibility each of us must take to ensure that others are not harassed. An excerpt is printed below (for the full reproduction, please see Chapter Eight):

How am I supposed to know what's unwelcome behaviour?

More often than not, if we pay attention, the message is clear. People show their disapproval in different ways:

- verbal responses such as: "no", "I don't like that", "your joke is not appreciated", etc.,
- physical responses such as pushing a hand away, moving away or leaving the room,
- facial expressions indicating discomfort or distress,
- nervous smiles or laughter,
- silence, such as not laughing at offensive jokes.

Sometimes these signs are not clear. You need to be sensitive to the possibility that others do not welcome your behaviour.

The courts do not always require a person to have verbally responded in order to prove that behaviour is unwelcome.

How can joking around or ribbing someone be considered harassment if I'm just having a little fun?

Humour can help relieve tension, reduce boredom and create a bond between people. Everyone can appreciate a good joke but not if it's told at someone else's expense. Remember that people may be sensitive about issues such as race, religion and gender. Use your judgement — if you don't know whether or not a joke will be appreciated, then don't tell it. If it's clear you have offended someone, apologize and don't repeat your behaviour. A single joke may not be considered harassment if it doesn't have a major impact.

. . . . .

If I complain, won't other people say I'm too uptight, that I can't take a joke?

If you are being harassed you have a right to stand up for yourself. Harassment is not a joke. It's a put down.

Harassment situations can be resolved confidentially, without wide knowledge. If you need advice on how to stop certain behaviour, talk to an advisor on a confidential basis.

In a separate section, the B.C. Hydro policy reviews steps employees can take to help prevent harassment. The steps are excerpted here:

What can employees do?

Prevention requires a willingness on the part of all employees to create a workplace free of harassment. Laws, regulations and procedures to deal with harassment are no substitute for respectful behaviour between all employees. Each of us can have a powerful impact on the environment in which we work. We can:

- Challenge harassment when it's happening. Assume that people want to treat others well and will respond positively.
- Refuse to participate in the more subtle forms of harassment. For example, refuse to laugh at harassment disguised as humour. Sometimes this is a bit awkward and takes courage but it's not so difficult after the first time.
- Support co-workers who are being harassed. Too often, people feel isolated and alone and they need support. But don't take over. Everyone has to make their own decisions.
- Speak up if we are harassed.
- Call on managers and union representatives to take action and to educate all employees.
- Check our own actions. Most of us do not harass others. If we do, it may be a result of insensitivity or not being sure what is appropriate, respectful workplace behaviour.
- Call an advisor to assist in dealing with the harassment.

The excerpt below is part of a publication prepared by the Saskatchewan Human Rights Commission, called "Erasing Racism". It gives some concrete examples of ways in which individuals can work toward ridding the workplace or classroom of racial harassment. Many of the steps can be easily translated into sexual, disability, religious, sexual orientation, age or even personal harassment.

Start supporting victims of racial harassment.

Tell the perpetrator that the comment or action is offensive and hurtful, to the victim and to you. This way, racists will be more likely to think twice about repeating this kind of negative behaviour.

Let's say your co-worker thinks it's funny to tell jokes about people of Chinese ancestry. Another employee is from Hong Kong and is upset by the "humour." Don't laugh at another's humiliation. Let the jokester know the story makes you uncomfortable. If you laugh or smile, you show your approval and become equally to blame for encouraging racism.

Or, you see a group of white students teasing and pushing a black classmate around in the lunchroom. Either tell them to stop, or let your teacher, guidance counsellor or principal know about the incident. Make sure some action is taken.

Racist graffiti and hate literature have become commonplace in many workplaces, particularly with the development of the fax machine which has eased the spread of hundreds of racist documents around the world. These materials continue to find their way into our schools too.

Racial slurs expressed in pictures or in writing are harassment. It's hurtful and demeaning.

If anything like this appears in your office, find out right away who is responsible. Tell them the material is offensive and that they've violated human rights law. Or, tell your supervisor. Management is legally required to ensure a harassment-free workplace.

Likewise, if you see this kind of harassment in your school, tell your teacher, or someone else in authority.

Reprinted by permission of the Saskatchewan Human Rights Commission.

These excerpts from B.C. Hydro and the Saskatchewan Human Rights Commission provide some sound advice for ways in which individuals can actively address harassment. The suggestions are straightforward, but could prove somewhat difficult for some individuals to effect. If an employee has questions about the best approach to take in a given situation he or she should be able to speak to an employee designated within the organization to deal with harassment issues. The designated employee should be able to offer support and perhaps some other effective approaches for an employee to follow.

SUPERVISORS AND MANAGERS

In B.C. Hydro's harassment policy (fully cited in Chapter Eight), supervisors and managers are given specific duties to prevent harassment. This is an excellent approach to ensure that the anti-harassment message is carried throughout an organization. This policy states:

What must supervisors and managers do?

Managers are obligated to implement and uphold company policies regarding human rights in the workplace.

The daily actions of supervisors and managers are critical in preventing harassment. They must:

A. *Be proactive*
- stop harassment that occurs,
- challenge inappropriate comments and jokes,
- remove offensive visual materials,
- provide support to employees who are harassed,
- encourage employees who are being harassed to make complaints, and
- approach employees sensitively if there are grounds to suspect that harassment is occurring.

B. *Educate*
- inform all employees about harassment and their rights and responsibilities, and
- ensure that new employee orientation includes information about the harassment policy and procedures.

C. *Implement policy in their immediate area*
- act quickly to implement discipline or other recommendations which result from harassment investigations, and
- follow up to ensure that harassment has stopped.

D. *Ensure safety*
- be sensitive to the needs of employees working alone.

E. *Model appropriate behaviour*
- act appropriately towards all employees (harassment is often part of a larger pattern of disrespectful attitudes in the workplace), and
- let all employees know that you will not participate in, tolerate or ignore harassment behaviour.

For further suggestions, the following section also focuses on steps for supervisors and managers as representatives of the employer.

STEPS EMPLOYERS CAN TAKE

Employers are in an excellent position to take steps to deal with harassment in the workplace. First, they have the ability to set a written and publicized code of conduct for their employees, from workplace safety to dress codes to hours of work. A workplace harassment policy should be one of the rules that make up part of this written code of conduct.

In addition, and perhaps even more importantly, employers set the tone for a workplace with unwritten rules or for the way in which they enforce the written ones. Employers create a certain environment or culture through their actions and their inaction. In this context it will be obvious to employees that some behaviour is not tolerated, that other behaviour is condoned or even encouraged, and still other behaviour is rewarded. These are the unwritten rules of the workplace. Any employee who works for an employer for a period of time becomes aware of this code of conduct as well as the written rules.

Employers can promote respect for all employees in the workplace by using both of these channels, the formal, written, public route and the unpublicized, unwritten route. The first route requires the development and implementation of a strong harassment policy.

The second route requires that the policy is taken seriously by the chief executive officer, other executives, the managers and supervisors. It also requires consistent, fair enforcement of the policy. This does not mean creating an environment where fun and friendship cannot exist. In fact, it should mean the opposite. Sending a clear message through one's actions that harassment will not be tolerated should allow employees to relax and feel comfortable in their social interaction with co-workers. It should also allow them to feel confident that they will be able to perform to the best of their abilities and they will be judged at work on that basis.

It is perhaps the second area that is the most difficult to maintain. It requires consistency. It requires employers and their representatives at all levels to walk the talk or be perceived as hypocrites. The inappropriate comment or joke or the quick slap on the buttocks of a member of the opposite sex can undermine a workplace harassment policy that has taken a great deal of work to develop. This message needs to be conveyed and understood by all levels of management within an organization.

Several human rights commissions across Canada have provided advice to employers on steps they should take to prevent harassment and to avoid liability. The relevant portions of these publications are printed below. The publications are reprinted in their entirety in Chapter Ten.

The Saskatchewan Human Rights Commission has published these steps that employers can take:

If you are an employer ...

It's up to the employer to provide a discrimination-free workplace. Whether they are aware of sexual harassment or not, employers are responsible for the actions of management and supervisory personnel, and for the harassment by non-supervisory personnel in certain circumstances.

If, for example, an employee is harassed by a fellow employee and the employer knows about it but doesn't intervene, the employer may also be at fault.

Employers can achieve a discrimination-free workplace by:
- establishing a code of conduct
- establishing an anti-harassment policy
- setting up a confidential complaint process for victims of sexual harassment
- making sure all employees know the policy by posting it, putting it in memo form, or in the company newsletter
- letting employees know that penalties will follow sexual harassment, including written or verbal reprimands, suspension, and termination
- establishing a monitoring system

In Manitoba, the Human Rights Commission compiled these steps for employers in its Fact Sheet (of April 18, 1988):

What should you do?

An employer, landlord or service provider should take active steps to discourage harassment in the workplace, and must do so if they are aware, or ought to be aware, that harassment is occurring in their place of business.

Take all reasonable steps to prevent harassment ... to terminate harassment once it has occurred .... to mitigate or avoid the effect of harassment.

Such reasonable steps may include:

- developing internal policies to deal with harassment
- communicating these policies to all employees
- informing the harasser that the behaviour will not be tolerated and that disciplinary action or dismissal may follow if the behaviour continues
- taking disciplinary action where appropriate
- providing protection and support for the victim
- contacting The Manitoba Human Rights Commission for assistance.

In New Brunswick, the Human Rights Commission suggests the following in its harassment publication:

How can employers prevent sexual harassment?

- Develop a sexual harassment policy that establishes a procedure for investigating complaints quickly, confidentially and impartially. It should ensure that action is taken against harassers and that victims are protected from reprisals.
- Post the sexual harassment policy and ensure that all employees are aware of it.
- Take action to eliminate sexist jokes.
- Remove sexist or indecent posters, graffiti and photos.
- Provide training on sexual harassment for managers and employees; emphasize the seriousness of the issue.

The Newfoundland Human Rights Commission has published the following guidelines:

And what you can do:

1. Send out a letter defining sexual harassment and your policy on it, to all staff and post it on employee bulletin boards.
2. Discuss sexual harassment in management and supervisory training sessions. Make supervisory personnel aware of the repercussions of sexual harassment and what it means to the work environment.
3. In orientation sessions with new employees, deal with the issue of sexual harassment and make it known that you will treat any complaints seriously.
4. Ensure that parties to complaints of sexual harassment are protected from reprisals from each other, or other workers, during the investigative process.

Here are some further, concrete steps that an employer can take from the Canadian Human Rights Commission. The following excerpt is from the Commission's "Harassment Casebook — Summaries of Selected Harassment Cases":

As an employer or provider of goods and services you have a responsibility to provide an environment that is free of harassment. You are also responsible for any act committed by any of your officers, directors, employees or agents in the course of their employment. This was made clear by a 1987 Supreme Court decision in the case of *Robichaud v. Treasury Board.*

If you, as an employer or as a provider of goods and services, have done everything possible to provide an environment free of harassment and react quickly and appropriately to harassment complaints, you will not be held responsible for the harassment. The examples which follow illustrate in more detail the three principles that should guide you.

Prevention. You can act diligently to prevent harassment by ensuring:
- there are no derogatory posters in the workplace;
- comments or jokes that insult or demean others on discriminatory grounds are known by all employees to be unacceptable;
- all staff are educated about what harassment consists of;
- there is a clear and well-publicized policy against harassment which includes the names of the individuals in your organization who have been trained to handle harassment complaints; and
- there is a procedure in place for dealing with complaints.

All these actions will help convey the message that you will not tolerate harassment.

Action. If anyone involved in the control of your organization, such as a supervisor or manager, learns that harassment may be going on and does nothing about it, and does not even bring it to the attention of someone responsible for dealing with such situations, the organization may be considered to have consented to the harassment. Your organization must investigate any allegation of harassment to try to find out what happened.

Correction. To establish that you did all you could to mitigate or avoid the effects of harassment, you must ensure that corrective measures are taken. These could include:

- issuing sanctions against the individual harasser, ranging from a written reprimand to mandatory counselling or even dismissal;
- compensating the person who has been harassed;
- ensuring the victim receives either an oral or written apology;
- providing training on human rights to all staff; and
- making sure that all employees have a copy of and clearly understand your harassment policy, including who to contact if they feel they are being harassed.

Reproduced with permission of the Minister of Public Works and Government Services, 1995.

In summary, here are the three important steps that all employers can take:

1. Draft a workplace policy. First, gather a good working group to develop the policy. If the organization has distinctly different work areas, services, or products, your policy will be much stronger if each of these groups is represented during the policy development process:

   See Chapter Seven for the ten basic elements of any effective workplace policy and then Chapter Eight for some examples of different policies. One note of caution — each organization is unique. Do not simply "borrow" a policy from another organization without first considering all the implications for your own workplace. Use one you like as a template and adjust it as required.

2. Publish the policy. Employees have to be aware of it and the issues involved if the policy is to be effective. No matter how good it is, the policy is useless if it is hidden from view and simply filed in the employee manual.

   Don't be overly concerned that some complaints will materialize just because a policy has been prepared and employees are told about it. This may well happen but these complaints do not appear from nowhere. They are live issues that must be addressed. They existed before the policy was introduced, the policy did not create them. Now the organization has the opportunity to deal with them before they become larger problems.

3. Conduct training. Training needs to occur for all levels of employees. The workplace policy should be introduced in conjunction with a training program that explains why the policy has been prepared, how it works and what its effects will be. This is discussed more fully below.

STEPS HARASSED EMPLOYEES CAN TAKE

The Saskatchewan Human Rights Commission has identified the effects of harassment on the employee at the receiving end:

How does the victim feel?

Victims of sexual harassment feel humiliated, ashamed, degraded, embarrassed, and angry.

Sexual harassment impairs job performance, decreases job satisfaction, and causes headaches, nervousness, insomnia and anxiety attacks.

It's also wasteful. When employees have to spend time and energy dealing with sexual harassment it takes time and energy away from the job. Sexual harassment often leads to absenteeism and high staff turnover.

Several of the harassment awareness publications issued by government authorities also provide guidance to individual employees who are harassed. These steps provide positive action for employees who may be feeling victimized. The Alberta Human Rights Commission included the following information:

What can a victim do?

Anyone who believes he or she has been sexually harassed should first make it clear to the offender and/or to a person in authority that such action is unwanted.

If the behaviour persists, or corrective action is not taken, a complaint may be filed with the Alberta Human Rights Commission. This must be done within *six months* of the alleged incident, or the Commission does not have the authority to investigate.

For the purposes of later investigation, a record should be kept of when the alleged incidents occurred, the nature of the behaviour, the names of any witnesses and any other information useful to the investigation.

In New Brunswick, the Human Rights Commission suggests the following:

What should I do if I am sexually harassed?

- Do not ignore the harassment; it will probably get worse if you do.
- Tell the harasser that the behaviour is unwelcome, either verbally or in writing.

If the harassment persists,

- Contact the Human Rights Commission for advice or to file a complaint.
- Record the details of every incident, including time, date, witnesses, exactly what each of you said and how it made you feel physically and emotionally.
- If possible, get support from employees and former employees who may have been witnesses or may have been harassed themselves.
- Avoid being alone with the harasser if possible.

The Community Legal Information Association of P.E.I. Inc. outlines background information education and action steps in its material which is presented in everyday language and sample workplace scenarios:

> Julia is feeling more and more uncomfortable with her co-worker Brian. In the firm in which they work, she and Brian have to work together developing funding proposals and carrying out projects. The problem is that Brian is always asking questions about her personal life and often makes teasing remarks of a sexual nature. When she tries to discourage him, he makes their teamwork very difficult, often not keeping her informed and making her appear incompetent in front of their clients.
>
> *Is this sexual harassment?*
>
> Yes it is. Sexual harassment is a discriminatory practice under the *Canadian Labour Code,* the *Canadian Human Rights Act,* the *Prince Edward Island Human Rights Act* and the *Employment Standards Act* of Prince Edward Island.
>
> All of these Acts give you the right to employment free of sexual harassment. The responsibility lies with the employer to see that it does not happen, and to take appropriate steps if it is reported.
>
> Sexual harassment is gender (or sex) based discrimination. Although it can happen to men, it happens primarily to women and it happens because they are women.
>
> . . . . .
>
> *What can Julia do?*
>
> Julia does not have to put up with this behaviour. She can inform her employer and if nothing is done to stop the harassment she can take her case to the Human Rights Commission. Julia should keep notes on every act of harassment that occurs, including a description of the act, times, dates, and witnesses.
>
> . . . . .

Many places of employment have a sexual harassment policy in place. They state very clearly what to do if you are being harassed in this way.

- Don't ignore it, it won't go away, probably it will just get worse.
- Understand that you do not have to put up with it.
- Inform the harasser. If the behaviour doesn't stop, inform your supervisor, union representative, or other appropriate person on staff.
- If nothing happens file a complaint with the Human Rights Commission or follow the other steps outlined in your workplace policy.
- Keep notes of every act of harassment with times, dates, description, and names of witnesses. This is **VERY IMPORTANT**.
- Finally share the information with your co-workers. Other workers may have been harassed too.

Finally, the Newfoundland Human Rights Commission gives this guidance to employees feeling harassed:

And what you should do:

1. Make it clear to the harasser that the conduct is unwelcome and unacceptable.
2. Document each case of sexual harassment i.e. time, date, place, person involved, description of the type of harassment, any witnesses. If there are witnesses, have them sign your documentation.
3. Check with co-workers to see if they have experienced similar harassment and document these cases.
4. Report all cases of sexual harassment to a person in a position of authority.
5. Use the legal protection available. Before you decide to leave your job because of sexual harassment, report the case to the Human Rights Commission and obtain advice on the proper action to take.
6. Remember, you do not have to tolerate sexual harassment. Say "no" firmly and indicate you will not be intimidated and that you will take whatever action is necessary to protect your rights.

The steps outlined above are fully reproduced in Chapter Ten.

DESIGNING YOUR OWN TRAINING SESSIONS

Training employees to recognize and react appropriately to harassment is critical. But how is this done?

There are several different ways to approach training employees about workplace harassment. The route an organization will follow might depend on:

- *Budget*

A tighter budget requires some creativity, so focus your efforts as much as possible. Decide the key points of the message you want heard and concentrate on them. Shorter sessions are usually less expensive and less time-consuming for the participants and facilitators.

- *Time constraints*

    Sometimes an organization might want its entire workforce to learn about the policy within the same time period. If the workforce is large and the sessions have to be conducted within a tight time frame, some approaches may not be appropriate.

- *Internal resources*

    If there are people with training skills already within the organization, include them in the development and possibly the delivery process as much as possible. Make sure they understand the nature of workplace harassment issues.

- *External resources*

    If external consultants can be used to conduct some or all of the training, disruption to the organization itself is kept to a minimum. They are already trained to deal with harassment issues and training. Also, external consultants can sometimes be more readily perceived as independent than internal employees if this is an issue. However the use of consultants will result in hard costs.

- *Make-up of the employee group*

    The average age, literacy level, education level, gender and racial mix of an employee group must all be considered when designing a training session. Think about the best way to present information. What would be the most effective approach to allow employees to understand the policy? If there is a high illiteracy level, presenting a copy of a written policy is pointless.

- *Geographic structure of the organization*

    Is the organization spread out across the country? If so, can several different people deliver the information or is one preferable to ensure a consistent message is received?

- *Particular harassment or potential harassment problems that have already happened or that may happen*

    Be sensitive to complaints that have been made or problem areas that exist. The problems should be addressed in a way that shows that the organization is taking them seriously without appearing to make the harassment policy a personal one designed to fix a particular department's, or a particular employee's, problem.

- *Number of employees*

    The size of the employee group is influential on the approach that will be effective and the budget that will be required. Videos have been used effectively for training large groups with trained facilitators, to introduce the sessions and lead a group discussion afterward.

    There is a broad range of training that can take place on the subject of workplace harassment. Some organizations have prioritized harassment training and set aside a sufficient part of their overall budget that allows in-depth, one- or two-day training for all employees to take place. Others, however, are faced with tighter financial constraints and can offer their employees a one-hour question-and-answer session with a trained facilitator. This still provides employees with an opportunity to learn about the policy and express any concerns or questions they may have.

    One effective approach is to target training at three levels:

1. *Employee sessions*

    These sessions include a general explanation of the policy for all employees. Often a new or revised policy is introduced at these sessions.

    Employees appreciate the opportunity to express doubts or even scepticism as well as ask questions about the policy or the reasons for its existence. Welcome the chance to dispel their doubts or at least to become aware of any potential trouble spots that quickly become very apparent during training sessions. This is the company's chance to learn whether the employees have any apprehensions or concerns about the policy.

    Don't be surprised when employees are initially unenthusiastic about the topic of workplace harassment. Ensure that employees feel comfortable asking any questions they may have about harassment or the policy. If a training session cannot be held for all employees, make sure that they know whom they can ask for more information. If confidentiality might be an issue for some employees, provide them with a convenient place to leave written, anonymous requests for general information and post responses on the bulletin board or in the company newsletter.

2. *Supervisor and manager training*

    These sessions explain the policy and the role of the supervisor and manager. Supervisors and managers can make or break the process of dealing with workplace harassment. They are central to ensuring that the workplace is free of harassment, or, if harassment does occur, that they understand how and why they are to respond. Often, a company's only possible defence to a complaint of harassment within its workplace is to respond effectively, quickly and appropriately. The individuals who are on the front line for response are the managers and supervisors. Organizations must make certain that these people understand how to react.

3. *Designated employees*

Some employees should be designated to receive complaints or questions about harassment. They must be provided with the information and support they need to fulfil this position. An in-depth session can cover all the above in greater detail, as well as give these selected employees the tools they need to administer the policy. They must receive enough training to understand the policy and the investigation or response process.

A session for these designated employees may focus on the policy and the contents of Chapter Nine, How to Investigate? Even if these employees are not going to be conducting formal investigations, they can benefit from the interview tips and listening skills discussed in that chapter.

CHAPTER SEVEN

What are the Basics of a Harassment Policy?

THE TEN BASIC ELEMENTS OF A POLICY

A workplace harassment policy must be carefully structured. Each policy should contain the ten essential elements described in this chapter. These components provide only a framework, however. Each policy must be different to make it work within its own workplace. Every workplace, even within the same industry, indeed, even within the same organization, can have a different environment, sometimes referred to as a corporate culture. The unique nature of the particular workplace must be taken into account when preparing a harassment policy. To be effective, the policy must be relevant to its own workplace.

Harassment policies do not work in a vacuum. They should be communicated to employees in conjunction with an education or awareness program. These policies may be seen by employees as a powerful aid to enable them to work without fear of harassment, or they may be perceived to be threatening and intrusive, or they may be seen as a great waste of time. Employees designated to deal with matters of harassment internally must receive the appropriate training to enable them to fulfil their mandate.

Check the legislation in your own jurisdiction before you begin preparing a workplace harassment policy. Some jurisdictions include specific definitions or defences that will apply whether they are included in the policy or not. The best approach may be to incorporate the legislative directives directly. Excerpts of the legislation are contained in the Appendix.

The federal workforce has been issued some very specific edicts about one form of harassment — sexual harassment. The *Canada Labour Code* contains several requirements that *must* be considered when a federally regulated company is developing a workplace harassment, or even just a sexual harassment, policy. One part of the Code requires that *every* federally regulated employer must have a policy statement on sexual harassment. It outlines the mandatory contents and publicity of the policy in section 247.4:

Policy statement by employer

(1) Every employer shall, after consulting with the employees or their representatives, if any, issue a policy statement concerning sexual harassment.

Contents of policy statement

(2) The policy statement required by subsection (1) may contain any term consistent with the tenor of this Division the employer considers appropriate but must contain the following:

- (a) a definition of sexual harassment that is substantially the same as the definition in section 247.1;
- (b) a statement to the effect that every employee is entitled to employment free of sexual harassment;
- (c) a statement to the effect that the employer will make every reasonable effort to ensure that no employee is subjected to sexual harassment;
- (d) a statement to the effect that the employer will take such disciplinary measures as the employer deems appropriate against any person under the employer's direction who subjects any employee to sexual harassment;
- (e) a statement explaining how complaints of sexual harassment may be brought to the attention of the employer;
- (f) a statement to the effect that the employer will not disclose the name of a complainant or the circumstances related to the complaint to any person except where disclosure is necessary for the purposes of investigating the complaint or taking disciplinary measures in relation thereto; and
- (g) a statement informing the employees of the discriminatory practices provisions of the *Canadian Human Rights Act* that pertain to rights of persons to seek redress under that Act in respect of sexual harassment.

Publicity

(3) Every employer shall make each person under the employer's direction aware of the policy statement required by subsection (1).

GENERAL STATEMENT (THE FIRST ELEMENT)

Each policy must include a statement of the organization's commitment to preventing harassment in the workplace. This should come from the most senior representative of the organization, the President or Chief Executive Officer. This provides a powerful display of the seriousness of the issue and of the level of commitment from the most senior level. A simple, brief statement may have the most impact.

The following extract is an example of a statement of principle from the Canadian Union of Public Employees Union. It was signed by Judy Darcy and Geraldine McGuire.

Equality Statement

Union solidarity is based on the principle that union members are equal and deserve mutual respect at all levels. Any behaviour that creates conflict prevents us from working together to strengthen our union.

As unionists, mutual respect, cooperation and understanding are our goals. We should neither condone nor tolerate behaviour that undermines the dignity or self-esteem of any individual or creates an intimidating, hostile or offensive environment.

Harassment means using real or perceived power to abuse or humiliate. Harassment should not be treated as a joke. The uneasiness and discomfort it creates are not feelings that help us grow as a union. Harassment focuses on the things that make us different instead of the things that bring us together like shared concerns about our families, decent wages, safe working conditions, fairness at work, and justice in society.

We believe that CUPE's policies and practices should reflect our commitment to equality. We urge members and staff to participate fully in CUPE activities mindful that all sisters and brothers deserve dignity, equality and respect.

Reprinted by permission of the Canadian Union of Public Employees.

DEFINITION (THE SECOND ELEMENT)

The policy must include a definition of harassment. If the human rights legislation in the jurisdiction of the workplace includes a definition, as in Manitoba, Ontario, New Brunswick, Nova Scotia and Newfoundland, that definition should be included, or at least the elements of the definition should be incorporated. For example, the definition in the Ontario, New Brunswick and Newfoundland human rights Acts is identical: "harassment" means engaging in a course of vexations comment or conduct that is known or ought reasonably to be known to be unwelcome.

In Manitoba, harassment is defined as including four possible courses of conduct. This should be reinforced or highlighted in a Manitoba workplace policy:

> s. 19(2) In this section, "harassment" means:
>
> > (a) a course of abusive and unwelcome conduct or comment undertaken or made on the basis of any characteristic referred to in subsection 9(2); or

> (b) a series of objectionable and unwelcome sexual solicitations or advances; or
>
> (c) a sexual solicitation or advance made by a person who is in a position to confer any benefit on, or deny any benefit to, the recipient of the solicitation or advance, if the person making the solicitation or advance knows or ought reasonably to know that it is unwelcome; or
>
> (d) a reprisal or threat or reprisal for rejecting a sexual solicitation or advance.

Although the above definition refers to sexual harassment only, it may be paraphrased to include the other grounds as well.

In Nova Scotia, some of the Manitoba possibilities appear again, together with some new language:

> s. 3(o) "sexual harassment" means
>
> (i) vexatious sexual conduct or a course of comment that is known or ought reasonably to be known as unwelcome,
>
> (ii) a sexual solicitation or advance made to an individual by another individual where the other individual is in a position to confer a benefit on, or deny a benefit to, the individual to whom the solicitation or advance is made, where the individual who makes the solicitation or advance knows or ought reasonably to know that it is unwelcome, or
>
> (iii) a reprisal or threat of reprisal against an individual for rejecting a sexual solicitation or advance.

Again, the legislated definition references only sexual harassment but could easily be re-worded to include the other protected grounds.

In the federal arena, companies that are federally regulated are subject to not only the *Canadian Human Rights Act* but also the *Canada Labour Code*. The Code included a definition of sexual harassment. It requires that this definition, or one substantially similar, be used in a mandatory sexual harassment policy.

> Sec. 247.1 In this Division, "sexual harassment" means any conduct, comment, gesture or contact of a sexual nature:
>
> (a) that is likely to cause offence or humiliation to any employee; or
>
> (b) that might, on reasonable grounds, be perceived by that employee as placing a condition of a sexual nature on employment or on any opportunity for training or promotion.

A definition modelled after the one provided by the Supreme Court of Canada in an earlier case also works well, particularly in jurisdictions that do not have definitions of harassment in their human rights legislation. In that case, the court reviewed the meaning of sexual harassment at length and within that context stated:

> ... sexual harassment in the workplace may be broadly defined as unwelcome conduct of a sexual nature that detrimentally affects the work environment or leads to adverse job-related consequences .... (*Janzen v. Platy Enterprises Ltd.*, [1989] 1 S.C.R. 1252, 10 C.H.R.R. D/6205 at page D/6227)

Working with that definition, a definition that could apply to all forms of harassment could be developed. For example:

> Workplace harassment is unwelcome conduct that has a negative impact on the workplace.

These general definitions are necessarily broad, perhaps to the point of vagueness. However, they will be supplemented by specific examples of behaviour that is harassment.

EXAMPLES (THE THIRD ELEMENT)

The general definition of "harassment" is a good starting point but requires elaboration. Employees and others will want more information about what it covers. Include a list of concrete examples in the policy. These should make sense in the workplace in question. Typical examples may include unwelcome touching, leering, jokes, posters and calendars. The examples included in publications prepared by human rights commissions in Canada include a laundry list of physical, verbal and visual practices. Any of these could be used. In particular, it is important to include some examples of visual and verbal behaviour because they can be the least well-known.

Examples are:

- comments or jokes that demean or belittle another individual;
- comments about a person's body, positive, negative or otherwise;
- comments about another's ethnic origin, race or colour;
- negative stereotyping;
- comments about sexual attractiveness, or about sexual unattractiveness;
- comments about sexual desires or practices;
- posters or calendars that could be offensive;
- inappropriate screen savers;
- offensive e-mail messages;
- lewd looks — elevator eyes, staring at body parts;
- assault;
- touching, patting, pinching;
- massaging;
- caressing.

APPLICATION (THE FOURTH ELEMENT)

Clearly outline the application and scope of the policy. Tell employees what it covers and to whom it applies. This will vary depending on the nature of the workplace. The scope of the policy should address the types of situations covered, for example, work-related travel, conferences, and so on. This section can also reference the grounds on which complaints can be made and the situations in which harassment can occur. If personal harassment is going to be covered, it must be stated. The courts will not interpret a harassment policy to automatically include personal harassment, only discriminatory harassment — that is, only harassment based on one of the protected grounds such as sex, race, sexual orientation and so on.

If employees are in contact with suppliers, repairers, couriers, customers, clients or other third parties, it should be stated that they are also protected from their harassment in addition to harassment from co-workers, or involving management or supervisory personnel.

WHO RECEIVES COMPLAINTS? (THE FIFTH ELEMENT)

Someone must be identified to be available to hear employee complaints and to respond to any questions they may have. The policy should clearly name the individuals available to receive inquiries and complaints. Where the individuals are employed within the organization, they must satisfy two important criteria: first, they must be sufficiently senior that others will recognize that they can do something about issues, and second, these employees must be accessible to others and not appear to be intimidating.

In addition to being a corporate matter, harassment is also a personal issue. Employees must feel comfortable approaching the employees designated to deal with harassment within the workplace. If not, the internal process will not be effective and employees will either wait until the incidents have reached a critical point, or they will simply bypass the internal process and proceed to an external human rights agency.

PROCESS (THE SIXTH ELEMENT)

Outline the step-by-step process that will be followed after an inquiry is made, or a complaint is lodged. Emphasize that the designated employees are able to respond to inquiries as well as complaints. They do not have to be consulted only when an employee wishes to make a formal complaint. This will help encourage employees to come forward even if they are uncertain about the idea of a formal complaint. The earlier that someone is able to intervene, the greater the chance of a successful and quick resolution. Advisors should be able to provide employees with the advice and support they need to be able to address some situations themselves.

Let employees know how long it will take for the process to be completed. Timeliness is very important in this context. Ideally, an internal process should include the following time lines:

Initial contact — 1 day following notification of complaint
Initial interviews — 1 week
Final determination — 2 weeks.

This is a tight time frame by any stretch. The designated employees will have to be able to adjust their schedules to accommodate this. However, nothing is to be gained by increasing the amount of time it takes to resolve a harassment complaint.

CONFIDENTIALITY (THE SEVENTH ELEMENT)

Provide an assurance of confidentiality and privacy for the individuals involved. Confidentiality cannot always be guaranteed, but assurances can be given that every effort will be made to respect confidences to the greatest extent possible. If your policy guarantees confidentiality, any subsequent investigation will be greatly hampered. It is difficult to make a full determination of the facts when you are unable to provide others with all the information. This does not mean however that full disclosure is necessary for everyone with whom you come into contact during an investigation. Information should be given to others only on a need-to-know basis. Also, there will be some circumstances where it will be unnecessary to disclose the identity of a complainant. For example, where an employee or even a group of employees have expressed some concerns regarding the conduct of another employee in their work group it is possible to approach that employee and simply state that, "there have been some concerns expressed about comments that were made by you about —." This approach can work where no formal complaint has been made. However, in the case of a formal complaint such an approach can make an employee feel the target of an ambush — asked to defend himself against accusations that are not fully understood by him.

PROHIBITION OF RETRIBUTION (THE EIGHTH ELEMENT)

Include a statement that retribution or retaliation in any form will not be tolerated. This is critical. If employees feel that they are vulnerable in any way, the process will be ineffective.

The statement prohibiting retribution will send two messages:

1. Employees will be protected from any further actions once they make a complaint; and
2. Harassers will be warned that there will be further consequences above and beyond those that result from the initial complaint if there is retaliation or retribution.

REMEDIES (THE NINTH ELEMENT)

Review possible remedies for employees who are harassed. If employees are entitled to leaves of absence while the dispute is being reviewed, this should be stated here. If a transfer is a possible option, this can be included, but it must be stressed that this would only be at the option of the harassed.

It must be clear that harassed employees will not be made to bear the brunt of a resolution of the complaint.

PENALTIES (THE TENTH ELEMENT)

Outline the potential consequences of harassment for the harasser. Give a range of penalties from warnings to discharge. These can simply be included in a laundry list fashion. Do not try to link up penalties with offences. It must be left to the decision-maker at the time to apply the appropriate penalty. Otherwise, unless the list is followed precisely each time there is a finding of harassment, an employer will not be able to rely on it. If the penalties are invoked in an inconsistent manner, they will be seen to be capricious and unfair.

However, the most severe of the penalties, "up to and including dismissal from employment", must be spelled out in the policy. In addition, case law suggests that this potential consequence must be brought to the employees' attention at training or awareness sessions regarding the policy. (See *Bannister v. General Motors of Canada Ltd.* (1994), 8 C.C.E.L. (2d) 281 (Ont. Gen. Div.).)

Although every incident of harassment is serious, not every incident will warrant termination. The full range of discipline available will vary with the workplace. If a workplace is unionized, progressive discipline can be an option in some cases.

CHAPTER EIGHT

What are Other Organizations Doing?

FIVE WORKPLACE HARASSMENT POLICIES — INTRODUCTION

The basic elements of workplace harassment policies provide a framework for the preparation of a policy. It is also helpful to take a look at what some other organizations are doing. How have they put these principles into words?

There are many different styles of policies. Some are very (overly) legalistic, others brief to the point of vagueness, while others include intricate processes where every possible nuance has been carefully thought out and committed to paper.

The following examples are provided to give a flavour of various policies already being used in different-sized organizations in different industries. The first two are reprinted on a no-names basis. The third, fourth and fifth were prepared by B.C. Hydro (from "Harassment Free — A Guide to Creating a Respectful Workplace"), the Alberta Human Rights Commission, and the Saskatchewan Women's Secretariat (from "Preventing Harassment — A Guide for Employers") respectively. Finally, some collective agreement clauses dealing with harassment issues and assembled by the Canadian Union of Public Employees are also reprinted here.

Review these policies and think about how they would have to be changed to fit a different organization. Each policy must be customized to its own workplace to make it work, but these samples provide a good starting point.

SMALL PROFESSIONAL FIRM (UNDER 100 EMPLOYEES)

HARASSMENT POLICY

A. *Policy Statement*

Our goal is to promote equal opportunity for all our employees and job applicants. To fulfil this goal we have prepared this policy and process to protect employees from discrimination, including harassment, on the basis of:

- age;
- religion;
- sex;
- sexual orientation;
- race, colour or place of origin;
- disability;
- marital or family status.

In addition, we will protect employees from general harassment that is not necessarily based on any of the protected grounds listed above, but is just nasty behaviour.

B. *What is Harassment?*

Workplace harassment is any form of unwelcome conduct that interferes with work performance and impacts on the employment relationship. Unwelcome conduct is often described as offensive or humiliating, endangering the employee's continued employment or opportunity for training or promotion, or undermining the employee's personal sense of dignity. For example, harassment includes:

- unnecessary physical contact;
- unwelcome sexual flirtation;
- inappropriate comments or jokes;
- name-calling or racial slurs;
- graffiti and posters.

Some examples of harassment might surprise you:

- Even the best intentioned "compliments" regarding a person's appearance, hair, clothes etc., if made on a repeated basis in the work environment, or during a formal business meeting, can set a person apart as different. These comments can undermine the person's credibility as a professional.

- A statement, expressing the belief that a person of a certain gender, race or ethnic background would not be suitable for a management position because traditionally members of that gender, race or ethnic background are too subservient or docile, is another example of harassment.

- An individual who sees another person receive unequal treatment or hears someone tell an offensive joke to another, may view the behaviour as poisoning the environment.

It is important to note that one does not have to be the person targetted by the comments or conduct to experience harassment.

C. Who Can You Talk To?

We have four advisors, selected by staff, available to discuss harassment issues with you:

> (List designated advisors here)

The above designated advisors will be able to answer any questions you may have about harassment and to discuss these conflicts informally with you without taking action.

Harassment questions and complaints are always kept as confidential as possible. All employees are protected from any form of reprisal taken because of a complaint.

D. What Will Happen?

The firm has adopted five steps to ensure that a thorough and consistent complaint investigation is performed. The advisor will:

1. determine what happened based on evidence gathered;
2. determine whether harassment occurred;
3. determine the appropriate action;
4. communicate findings to the parties involved; and
5. document all steps taken from the initiation to resolution.

Advisors are committed to conducting a thorough, objective and confidential investigation to resolve the situation. These procedures are not mandatory and are not intended to replace any person's right to file a complaint with the applicable provincial human rights commission.

In the workplace, employees encounter many persons who are not employees of the firm, for example, clients, external consultants, couriers, sales representatives. An employee who has been subjected to harassment by a person not employed by the firm is encouraged to discuss the matter with an advisor. The firm will support all employees in these circumstances.

MEDIUM-SIZED CORPORATION — NON-UNION ENVIRONMENT (ABOUT 1000 EMPLOYEES)

The company is committed to providing every employee a work environment that is free from any kind of discriminatory harassment. This policy covers each of the legally protected grounds — sex, race, religion, age, physical disability, mental disability, sexual orientation, marital or family status. Discriminatory harassment is defined as any unsolicited or unwelcome conduct based on the protected grounds that has adverse employment consequences for the employee.

A coercive form of harassment could be, for example, where an employee refuses to submit to a social or sexual demand and is penalized by loss of job, raise, or other employment benefit. However, less obvious forms of harassment may also constitute an abusive working environment. Examples are verbal abuse or threats, unwelcome remarks, discriminatory jokes, innuendoes or taunting displays of pornographic or offensive posters/pictures, practical jokes that cause awkwardness or embarrassment, unwelcome invitations or requests, staring or similar gestures, condescension or paternalism that undermines self-respect, and unnecessary physical contact.

The company will make every reasonable effort to ensure that no employee is subject to discriminatory harassment and will take disciplinary measures as it deems appropriate against any person who subjects any employee to discriminatory harassment. Retribution will not be tolerated.

Eligibility

Every employee has the right under the *Human Rights Act* to seek redress with respect to discriminatory harassment.

Application

This policy applies to all work-related activities between employees, and employees' interaction with third parties such as suppliers, service and delivery personnel, and members of the public.

Administration

Employees are encouraged to immediately communicate their feelings of discomfort with respect to unwelcome behaviour whenever it occurs. Employees are also encouraged to seek the assistance of their supervisor, if appropriate, to address an unsatisfactory work environment.

All formal complaints of discriminatory harassment should be brought to the attention of the Vice-President of Human Resources, or any Human

Resources Manager. The employee's identity and circumstances will be held in confidence until permission is given by the employee to disclose information for the purpose of investigation.

Remedies

The company's first objective will be to ensure that any harassment is addressed and action is taken to stop any further harassment from occurring. Consequent disciplinary measures for any person found to have breached the conditions of this policy will range from reprimands, suspensions, transfers and demotions to termination of employment.

LARGE CORPORATION — UNION ENVIRONMENT (MORE THAN 1000 EMPLOYEES)

INTRODUCTION

As part of our goal to be the most progressive employer in the province, B.C. Hydro recognizes the social, ethical and legal responsibilities for eliminating harassment in the workplace. We are committed to providing a work environment where all individuals are treated with dignity and respect.

In accordance with the B.C. *Human Rights Act*, all our employees must be free from discrimination on the basis of race, colour, ancestry, place of origin, religion, political belief, marital status, family status, age, physical or mental disability, sex and sexual orientation. In our workplace, any act of harassment is unacceptable and will not be tolerated.

As part of our commitment, we have adopted a policy, with input from our unions, to address workplace harassment. The policy defines workplace harassment, establishes a complaint procedure, and sets out corrective actions that will be taken if necessary.

Each of us is responsible for acting according to the spirit and intent of this policy. In doing so, we help to create a positive work environment that respects the diversity amongst us.

POLICY

I. Corporate policy statement

Purpose:

To promote a work environment in which all employees are treated with respect and dignity and are free from harassment in the workplace.

Policy:

B.C. Hydro is committed to providing its employees a work environment free from harassment where individuals treat one another with mutual respect and cooperation.

Procedure summary:

1.0 Application of policy

1.1 Each employee is responsible for conducting herself or himself within the spirit and intent of this policy and for contributing towards a work environment free from harassment.

1.2 Each manager will foster in her/his area a work environment where harassment is not tolerated and will take appropriate and timely action whenever she/he has actual knowledge of harassment. Harassment does not include actions taken in good faith while exercising managerial/supervisory rights and responsibilities.[*]

1.3 All complaints of harassment will be taken seriously and will be investigated in a confidential, impartial and timely manner. Harassment constitutes unacceptable behaviour which will not be tolerated and may be subject to discipline.

1.4 Retaliation against an individual because he/she has made a complaint of harassment or who has provided information is prohibited and shall be considered a form of harassment and shall be dealt with through this policy. Where, as a result of an investigation, it is determined that a complaint was made maliciously or with a specific intention to harm, formal disciplinary action may be taken against the complainant.

Nothing in this policy precludes existing rights under any applicable collective agreement.

II. To whom does the policy apply?

This policy applies to:

a) any employee, officer or director of Hydro, or
b) any person having a business relationship with Hydro (i.e. customer, contractor, consultant).

---

[*] For example, performance reviews.

This policy applies where there is a sufficient relationship between the questionable conduct or comment and the functioning of the workplace. In other words, the workplace is not confined strictly to the offices and buildings of Hydro; it also includes:

a) any location related to the business of Hydro (i.e. work yards, cafeterias, meeting rooms), and
b) other locations and situations (i.e. business travel) where the prohibited behaviour has or may be reasonably viewed as having a subsequent impact on the work relationship, environment or performance.

Conduct or comments which constitute harassment and occur in locations covered by this definition are subject to investigation under this policy.

Individuals external to Hydro who have a business relationship with Hydro and a complaint regarding harassment by a Hydro employee or contractor/consultant working for Hydro may access this policy through direct written application to the Vice-President (VP) of Human Resources.

DEFINITIONS

What is harassment?

Most people think of harassment as sexual in nature but it actually takes many forms including discriminatory and personal harassment.

Harassment is generally conduct or comment which a reasonable person would consider to be objectionable or unwelcome, serves no related work purposes and which:

a) detrimentally affects people within the work environment, or
b) has adverse job related consequences (such as reduced job security or a negative impact on career advancement).

Harassment may occur during one incident or over a series of incidents. Some actions may not be considered harassment unless repeated. For example, a single joke may not be considered harassment if it doesn't have a major impact.

For the purposes of our policy, harassment includes conduct or comment that constitutes discrimination under the B.C. *Human Rights Act* and sexual and personal harassment as defined on the following pages.

Physical and sexual assault, or threats of violence directed towards you, your family and your possessions are criminal matters and should also be referred directly to your local police department.

A. *Discrimination*

Any objectionable or unwelcome conduct or comment in respect to:

- age
- ancestry
- birthplace
- colour
- conviction for an offense
- family status (parent-child)
- marital status
- mental disability
- physical disability
- political belief
- race
- religion
- sex
- sexual orientation

Examples:

- unwanted actions, derogatory or demeaning comments, jokes or slurs
- derogatory or demeaning posters, pictures, cartoons, graffiti, or drawings
- innuendoes, taunting or ostracizing a co-worker/employee

B. *Sexual harassment*

Sexual harassment is unwelcome comment or conduct of a sexual nature in the workplace when the comment or conduct is accompanied by one or more of the following:

- a reward or the expressed or implied promise of reward for compliance,
- a reprisal, or the expressed or implied threat of reprisal for refusing to comply,
- the actual denial of opportunity or the expressed or implied threat of the denial of opportunity for refusal to comply, or
- the intention or the effect of creating an intimidating, poisoned or offensive environment.

Examples:

- unwelcome remarks, questions, jokes, innuendo or taunting about a person's body or sex, including sexist comments or sexual invitations
- verbal abuse or threats of a sexual nature

- leering, staring or making sexual gestures
- display of pornographic or other sexual materials in the form of degrading pictures, graffiti, cartoons or sayings
- unwanted physical contact such as touching, patting, pinching, or hugging
- intimidation, threat or physical assault of a sexual nature
- sexual advances with actual or implied work related consequences

This definition of sexual harassment is not intended to inhibit interactions or relationships based on mutual consent or normal social contact between employees.

C. Personal harassment

Personal harassment is objectionable conduct or comment, directed towards a specific person, which serves no legitimate work purpose and has the effect of creating an intimidating, humiliating, hostile or offensive work environment.

Examples:

- threats, bullying, coercion
- actual or threatened physical assault
- verbal assault, taunting or ostracizing
- malicious gestures or actions

QUESTIONS & ANSWERS

Some common questions answered

How am I supposed to know what's unwelcome behaviour?

More often than not, if we pay attention, the message is clear. People show their disapproval in different ways:

- verbal responses such as: "no", "I don't like that", "your joke is not appreciated", etc.,
- physical responses such as pushing a hand away, moving away or leaving the room,
- facial expressions indicating discomfort or distress,
- nervous smiles or laughter,
- silence, such as not laughing at offensive jokes.

Sometimes these signs are not clear. You need to be sensitive to the possibility that others do not welcome your behaviour.

The courts do not always require a person to have verbally responded in order to prove that behaviour is unwelcome.

How can joking around or ribbing someone be considered harassment if I'm just having a little fun?

Humour can help relieve tension, reduce boredom and create a bond between people. Everyone can appreciate a good joke but not if it's told at someone else's expense. Remember that people may be sensitive about issues such as race, religion and gender. Use your judgement — if you don't know whether or not a joke will be appreciated, then don't tell it. If it's clear you have offended someone, apologize and don't repeat your behaviour. A single joke may not be considered harassment if it doesn't have a major impact.

What if I only touched someone once and I didn't intend to offend? Will I be guilty of sexual harassment?

No, if it isn't repeated and the impact is minor. More than anything, people who are harassed want the behaviour to stop. If you didn't intend to offend, apologize and be willing to change your behaviour. The key is not to do it again.

However, a single incident can be considered sexual harassment if it has significant impact on the person. Under the human rights law, lack of intent to harass is not considered a defense. The courts are not interested in what a harasser "intended". They are concerned with the impact of the action on the person who has been harassed.

The key is to be responsible. Be aware of the potential effect of your actions on others.

Are friendly touching and "horsing around" okay?

Some people enjoy non-sexual touching. But if touch is not welcome then it isn't appropriate or friendly. Some people dislike all forms of physical contact and others feel pressured or offended by touching from someone who has authority over them. Still others welcome a friendly hug at an appropriate time.

Remember too that some cultures have different customs regarding touch. For example, while a handshake or hug may be considered an appropriate greeting in some cultures, in others these actions may be taken as offensive.

Can I ask someone for a date?

Some people may welcome an invitation to socialize. But pressuring someone for a date after they've clearly refused is not acceptable.

Is it okay to become romantically involved with a co-worker?

An individual's personal life is not the employer's concern and job decisions must be based solely on work-related performances and abilities. To do anything else is discrimination. However, there is a possibility of conflict of interest, particularly when a relationship exists between a supervisor and a co-worker. In this situation, regardless of how impartial all business judgements are, there may be the suspicion of special favours.

If I complain won't other people say I'm too uptight, that I can't take a joke?

If you are being harassed you have a right to stand up for yourself. Harassment is not a joke. It's a put down.

Harassment situations can be resolved confidentially, without wide knowledge. If you need advice on how to stop certain behaviour, talk to an advisor on a confidential basis.

Isn't it too risky to report? I could be isolated at work; it could affect my career.

Harassment cases are often not reported. Many people choose to remain silent because they fear publicity, not being taken seriously, or retaliation from supervisors or co-workers. That's why our harassment policy has been introduced.

Hydro takes your concerns seriously and has provided for confidential support and advice for anyone with questions and concerns through the Harassment Advisory Resource Line.

What is the role of Hydro's Security Department when dealing with harassment in the workplace?

If you have concerns for your personal safety in the workplace you can contact the Security Department for assistance when dealing with the situation. Requests for harassment investigations should be referred to the Harassment Free Workplace program coordinator through the Harassment Free Advisory Resource Line.

PREVENTION

We all have a responsibility to stop harassment. The best way to stop harassment is to prevent it. This section reviews the roles each of us has with respect to prevention.

I. As an employer, what is Hydro doing?

Hydro is demonstrating its commitment to creating a workplace free from harassment by:

- making a strong, publicized commitment to a harassment free workplace,

- having a policy defining harassment and describing unacceptable behaviour,
- having effective and confidential procedures for dealing with harassment complaints, and
- providing an awareness education program for all employees and managers.

II. What must supervisors and managers do?

Managers are obligated to implement and uphold company policies regarding human rights in the workplace.

The daily actions of supervisors and managers are critical in preventing harassment. They must:

A. Be proactive

- stop harassment that occurs,
- challenge inappropriate comments and jokes,
- remove offensive visual materials,
- provide support to employees who are harassed,
- encourage employees who are being harassed to make complaints, and
- approach employees sensitively if there are grounds to suspect that harassment is occurring.

B. Educate

- inform all employees about harassment and their rights and responsibilities, and
- ensure that new employee orientation includes information about the harassment policy and procedures.

C. Implement policy in their immediate area

- act quickly to implement discipline or other recommendations which result from harassment investigations, and
- follow up to ensure that harassment has stopped.

D. Ensure safety

- be sensitive to the needs of employees working alone.

E. Model appropriate behaviour

- act appropriately towards all employees (harassment is often part of a larger pattern of disrespectful attitudes in the workplace), and
- let all employees know that you will not participate in, tolerate or ignore harassment behaviour.

III. What can employees do?

Prevention requires a willingness on the part of all employees to create a workplace free of harassment. Laws, regulations and procedures to deal with harassment are no substitute for respectful behaviour between all employees. Each of us can have a powerful impact on the environment in which we work. We can:

- Challenge harassment when it's happening. Assume that people want to treat others well and will respond positively.
- Refuse to participate in the more subtle forms of harassment. For example, refuse to laugh at harassment disguised as humour. Sometimes this is a bit awkward and takes courage but it's not so difficult after the first time.
- Support co-workers who are being harassed. Too often, people feel isolated and alone and they need support. But don't take over. Everyone has to make their own decisions.
- Speak up if we are harassed.
- Call on managers and union representatives to take action and to educate all employees.
- Check our own actions. Most of us do not harass others. If we do, it may be a result of insensitivity or not being sure what is appropriate, respectful workplace behaviour.
- Call an advisor to assist in dealing with the harassment.
- Become aware of our impact on others by listening to what co-workers say and learn to read "no" in body movements and facial expressions. We can also ask ourselves:
    - Is there anything in my behaviour that could offend, humiliate or degrade someone else?
    - Would I act or speak this way to someone about whom I care?

If we do offend without intending, we can try to understand why the other person is offended. We can apologize for causing hurt. We've all likely experienced or witnessed some type of harassment. We can learn about the impact of our behaviour on others and we can change.

Let's all share in promoting a work environment which is respectful!

Reprinted by permission of B.C. Hydro.

SAMPLE SEXUAL HARASSMENT POLICY FROM THE ALBERTA HUMAN RIGHTS COMMISSION

SAMPLE SEXUAL HARASSMENT POLICY

This sexual harassment policy is intended to be a sample only. It is not intended to reflect the needs of all employers. Rather it is meant to provide employers with a general guideline for the major provisions which should be included in an effective policy in order to make it sound, workable, accepted and used. Employers will need to adapt this policy or create entirely separate policies which best suit their individual organizations.

The Alberta Human Rights Commission can help develop or review your sexual harassment policy.

Sample: Alpha Company

Alpha Company, in co-operation with our unions, is committed to a healthy, harassment-free work environment for all our employees. To this extent, Alpha Company has developed a company-wide policy intended to prevent sexual harassment of its employees and to deal quickly and effectively with any incident that might occur.

Definition of Sexual Harassment

"Sexual harassment, being discrimination on the grounds of gender, is a violation of the *Individual's Rights Protection Act*. Unwanted sexual advances, unwanted request for sexual favours, and other unwanted verbal or physical conduct of a sexual nature constitute sexual harassment when:

1. Submission to such conduct is made either explicitly or implicitly a term of or condition of an individual's employment,
2. Submission to or rejection of such conduct by an individual affects that individual's employment."

Sexual harassment can include such things as pinching, patting, rubbing or leering, "dirty" jokes, pictures or pornographic materials, comments, suggestions, innuendoes, requests or demands of a sexual nature.

The behaviour need not be intentional in order to be considered sexual harassment. It is offensive and in many cases it intimidates others. It will not be tolerated within our company.

A) Procedure

If you are being sexually harassed:

1. Tell the individual his/her behaviour is unwelcome and ask him/her to stop.

2. Keep a record of incidents (date, times, locations, possible witnesses, what happened, your response). You do not have to have a record of events in order to file a complaint, but a record can strengthen your case and help you remember details over time.
3. File a complaint. If, after asking the harasser to stop his/her behaviour, the harassment continues, report the problem to one of the following individuals:

   a) Department Manager
   b) Director of Personnel
   c) Union Representative

You also have the right to contact the Alberta Human Rights Commission to file a complaint of sexual harassment and, if circumstances warrant it, the police to file a charge of assault.

B) Dealing with a Complaint

1. Once a complaint is received, it will be kept strictly confidential. An investigation will be undertaken immediately and all necessary steps taken to resolve the problem. If a complaint is filed through the union as a grievance, a meeting will be held with the union representative before and after the investigation.
2. The complainant and the alleged harasser will both be interviewed as will any individuals who may be able to provide relevant information. All information will be kept in confidence.
3. If the investigation reveals evidence to support the complaint of sexual harassment, the harasser will be disciplined appropriately. Discipline may include suspension or dismissal, and the incident will be documented in the harasser's file. No documentation whatsoever will be placed on the complainant's file where the complaint is filed in good faith, whether the complaint is upheld or not.
4. If the investigation fails to find evidence to support the complaint, there will be NO documentation concerning the complaint placed in the file of the alleged harasser.
5. Regardless of the outcome of a sexual harassment complaint made in good faith, the employee lodging the complaint, as well as anyone providing information, will be protected from any form of retaliation by either co-workers or superiors. This includes demotion, unwanted transfer, denial of opportunities within the company, as well as harassment of the individual as a result of her/his having made a complaint or having provided evidence regarding the complaint.

C) Responsibility of Management

It is the responsibility of a director, manager, or any person within this company supervising one or more employees to take immediate and appropriate action to report or deal with incidents of sexual harassment whether brought to their attention or personally observed. Under no circumstance should a legitimate complaint be dismissed or downplayed nor should the complainant be told to deal with it personally.

Alpha Company seeks to provide a safe, healthy and rewarding work environment for its employees. *Sexual harassment will not be tolerated within this company!* If you feel you are being sexually harassed, contact us. We want to hear from you.

Note: A complaint must be filed with the Alberta Human Rights Commission within six months of the alleged incident.

Reprinted by permission of the Alberta Human Rights Commission.

SAMPLE POLICY FROM THE SASKATCHEWAN WOMEN'S SECRETARIAT

SAMPLE POLICY ON HARASSMENT

Statement of Commitment

_____ is committed to providing a safe, positive work environment where everyone is treated with respect and dignity.

Harassment in the workplace is unacceptable and against the law. It will not be tolerated in any form.

Definition of Harassment

Harassment is any unwanted conduct that offends or humiliates.

Harassment is prohibited on the following grounds: race, creed, religion, colour, sex, marital status, sexual orientation, family status, mental and physical disability, physical size or weight, age, nationality, ancestry or place of origin, or the receipt of public assistance.

It may be verbal, physical, visual or psychological. It can include but is not limited to:

- jokes that cause awkwardness or embarrassment
- display of racist, sexist or other offensive material
- sexually suggestive or obscene comments or gestures
- offensive sexual advances and propositions

- unwanted physical contact such as touching, patting or pinching
- verbal abuse, threats or intimidation
- physical assault, including sexual assault

Employer Responsibility

The employer shall ensure that no employee is subjected to harassment, whether it is from a supervisor, co-worker, or non-employee such as a client or customer.

Employee Responsibility

No employee shall participate in or encourage the harassment of another worker.

Coverage

This policy covers all employees at all levels. Applicants and candidates for employment are also covered.

Harassment will not be tolerated in any work-related setting, such as work-related conferences, seminars, travel and social events.

Complaint Procedure

Informal Options

An employee is encouraged to consider the following informal options:

- raise the issue with the person whose behaviour is a problem. This could be done verbally or in writing
- inform a supervisor or manager of the problem and ask him or her to informally discuss the situation with the alleged harasser.

Formal Options

If informal options are inappropriate or unsuccessful, an employee can file a formal complaint with one of the following people:

- employer
- any supervisor/manager
- shop steward (where applicable)
- or any of the following people designated by the employer:

_____   _____

_____   _____

Dealing with a Formal Complaint

Confidentiality

Any complaint of harassment will be kept in confidence, except as is necessary to investigate and resolve the situation.

Investigation

An investigation will be undertaken immediately. The alleged harasser will be promptly notified of the complaint.

The complainant and the alleged harasser will both be interviewed along with any individuals who may be able to provide relevant information.

Discipline

If the investigation reveals evidence to support the complaint of harassment, the harasser will be disciplined appropriately. Discipline may range from a verbal reprimand to suspension or dismissal, and the incident will be documented in the harasser's file.

Documentation

If the investigation fails to find evidence to support the complaint, there will be no documentation concerning the complaint placed in the file of the alleged harasser.

Retaliation

Retaliation against any individual for reporting harassment or providing information will not be tolerated.

Appeal Process

Within 120 days, either the complainant or the respondent may make a written request that the investigation be reviewed for thoroughness. The request must state what aspect of the investigation is inadequate. The request must be submitted to _____, who will determine if the investigation is to be re-opened in order to address concerns raised.

Other Options

This policy is meant to provide an effective redress mechanism. However, every employee also has the right to file a complaint with an outside agency, such as a Human Rights Commission or the Occupational Health and Safety Division, Saskatchewan Labour.

HANDLING A COMPLAINT: INFORMAL AND FORMAL OPTIONS

The first step in handling a complaint is to fully inform the complainant of their options and the possible outcomes of each. This includes informing unionized employees of their right to representation by their union.

An effective harassment policy provides informal and formal options for addressing complaints. Your responsibilities will vary depending on which mechanism is used.

Informal Complaints

The procedure for handling an informal complaint depends on whether or not the alleged harasser is identified by the complainant.

Informal complaints are those complaints which are brought to management's attention but which are not written and do not necessarily result in an investigation.

Informal procedures are often an effective and less costly means of dealing with less serious harassment situations. Most victims prefer not to take formal action, they just want the harassment to stop.

If the alleged harasser is not named, you may offer to handle the complaint by arranging for educationals for all staff.

This could include:

- workshops, videos or written information on the prevention of harassment
- staff meeting discussions and a review of your policy

If the alleged harasser is named, he or she must be informed of the concern and be provided with an opportunity to respond. This is known as "duty to the accused", and it is a legal responsibility of the employer.

In this case, you may offer to handle the informal complaint by arranging for:

- separate informal discussions between the supervisor and the complainant, and the supervisor and the respondent
- subject to the agreement of both parties, a facilitated meeting between the complainant and the respondent. The meeting should be facilitated by a mutually acceptable individual and allow the complainant and the respondent to address concerns about one another's behaviour. The facilitator may be someone from your workplace or you may consider hiring a trained mediator.

At any point in the informal complaint process, either the complainant or the respondent may choose to move to a formal complaint procedure and request an investigation.

Formal Complaints

Options for handling a formal complaint could include mediation or investigation.

A formal complaint is written and signed by the complainant. It should contain the following information:

- name of complainant
- home and work phone numbers
- location of workplace and department
- nature of complaint: racial, sexual, disability, etc.
- alleged harasser's name
- details of complaint — description of behaviour or incidents, what was said, date and location, circumstances surrounding incident and names of witnesses

Once a formal complaint has been received, it is essential to respond in a timely manner.

The first step is to promptly inform the alleged harasser of the complainant's concerns. This should include a copy of the written complaint.

Mediation

The goal of mediation is not to determine guilt or innocence, but rather to bring together the complainant and the alleged harasser in order to develop a mutually acceptable resolution. The decision to use mediation must be made by **both** the complainant and the alleged harasser.

It is important to assign a trained and impartial mediator. Keep in mind that should mediation be unsuccessful, an investigation of the complaint must be completed by someone other than the mediator.

Almost 48 per cent of women who are harassed lose their jobs. They are either fired or forced to quit because of intolerable working conditions.

— Ontario Women's Directorate

Guidelines for Conducting an Investigation

Ideally, the person assigned to investigate the complaint should be someone whose impartiality will not be in question. For example, if possible, do not assign someone to investigate their own co-workers. In some cases, it may be most appropriate to arrange for someone outside the workplace to investigate.

The investigator should:

- interview the complainant, the alleged harasser and potential witnesses
- take notes during every interview
- determine whether others have experienced similar problems
- assure confidentiality, as much as is possible
- prepare a written report, which includes a summary of the allegations, substance of witness statements tentative findings.

A copy of this report should be provided to the complainant and the alleged harasser. Both parties should have an opportunity to respond in writing to the investigator.

Following this, the investigator should prepare a final report including a detailed description of the findings and recommended course of action. All materials surrounding the investigation should be retained, pending any further action, such as an appeal or a human rights investigation.

Reaching a Conclusion in Your Workplace

There are some details of the investigation process that will be specific to each workplace. Consider the following questions:

- *For those cases which go to investigation:*
  - Who will receive a copy of the final report?
  - Who will make a final and binding decision regarding whether or not harassment occurred?

In many workplaces, there will be several people who could handle this responsibility, i.e. director of human resources, CEO, president, board chairperson. Wherever possible, it is best to assign this role to someone whose objectivity will not be in question.

- Who will decide what disciplinary action will be taken?
- Who will implement the disciplinary action?
- How long will the material surrounding the investigation be retained?

- *For all complaints, whether formal or informal:*
  - What information, if any, will be included in personnel files and under what circumstances?
  - How will you ensure that confidentiality is maintained?

- Who will follow-up with the complainant to ensure the harassing behaviour has stopped and to allow for any subsequent concerns to be addressed?

When All is Said and Done...

When a case of harassment is handled fairly, it can have a therapeutic effect on the workplace.

- For complainants, it offers the opportunity to have their concerns addressed.
- For harassers, it establishes guidelines for acceptable behaviour.
- For others in the workplace, it may clear the air and restore harmony.

What if Someone Complains?

- *Take the complaint seriously*
- *Listen respectfully*
- *Encourage the complainant to talk about the situation frankly*
- *Keep in mind how difficult it may have been to complain*
- *Ensure the complainant has input into how the problem will be solved*

Complainants may choose to raise the issue with the person whose behaviour is a problem. However, under no circumstances should they be required to confront the harasser as a means of resolving the situation.

Reprinted by permission of the Saskatchewan Women's Secretariat.

UNION CLAUSES

Unions have been instrumental in addressing workplace harassment issues for their members. The Canadian Union of Public Employees has prepared a fact sheet on workplace harassment that outlines several different clauses on many different harassment issues. Each of these clauses provides a good example of a working clause on a particular topic. The following excerpt is from "The Fact Sheet — Workplace Harassment" written by Cynthia Wishart, a senior CUPE equal opportunities officer.

THE FACT SHEET — WORKPLACE HARASSMENT

Some collective agreements provide a broad-based "anti-discrimination" clause and others simply incorporate the provision of the *Human Rights Code* by reference only. Though limited in number, some collective agreements do have a specific clause on sexual harassment. Those clauses normally prohibit sexual harassment of employees by their supervisors and/or co-workers.

For example, a collective agreement between Klinic Inc. (Manitoba) and CUPE Local 2348 specifically makes sexual harassment of co-workers a "just cause" for disciplinary action.

> A complaint of sexual harassment made against an employee shall be reported within five (5) days and upon investigation shall be cause for disciplinary action to be taken.

However, a collective agreement between the Place Riel Society and Local 1975 goes a step further and prohibits sexual harassment even by clients:

> Employees who are being subjected to client harassment will draw this to the attention of the supervisor, who will be required to deal with the problem immediately.

The normal grievance procedure, due to the sensitive nature of sexual harassment, has been found ineffective. Thus, the parties have attempted to provide different procedures and special remedies for sexual harassment grievances which may appear to be unusual in ordinary labour-management settings. Some of those provisions include:

1. *Confidentiality:*

   Most collective agreements provide that a grievance of sexual harassment shall be processed with strict confidentiality. One contract states:

   "Both parties agree that all proceedings and results thereof will be dealt with in the strictest confidence."

   To keep strict confidentiality, another collective agreement provides that "the complainant may elect to be present with or without a union representative, at any meeting where the employer is taking disciplinary action against the harasser." (Klinic Inc. (Manitoba) and CUPE Local 2348)

2. *Joint investigation:*

   Some collective agreements provide for a joint investigation of a harassment complaint by a team composed of the employer and the union representatives. (Government of Province of B.C. and BCGEU)

3. *Burden of proof:*

   Some collective agreements provide that "in the case of a complaint of sexual harassment, the onus shall be on the alleged harasser and not on the complainant to disprove the complaint." (Saskatchewan Association of Human Rights and CUPE Local 3012)

4. *Harasser to be transferred and not the victim:*

   Sexual harassment clauses in collective agreements normally provide that "in a case where sexual harassment may result in the transfer of an employee, it shall be the harasser who is transferred and the victim shall not be transferred against his or her will." (Town of Elliot Lake and CUPE Local 170)

5. *Disciplinary action against the harasser:*

   Some collective agreements provide that "the employer undertakes to discipline any person employed by it who engages in sexual harassment of another employee." (School District of North Vancouver and CUPE Local 389)

Other agreements go a step further and provide that an alleged harasser shall not be entitled to grieve disciplinary action taken by the employer which is consistent with the decision of the Deputy Minister or the panel. (Master agreement between the Government of B.C. and BCGEU)

6. *Leave with pay to the victim of sexual harassment:*

   One collective agreement provides for seven (7) days' leave with pay to the victim of sexual harassment and three (3) months' leave to a victim of sexual assault. (Canadian Federation of Students and CUPE Local 1281)

7. *Arbitrator empowered to impose a fine on the harasser:*

   Some collective agreements authorize an arbitration board to impose a financial penalty against the harasser. Further, the financial penalty collected from the harasser is to be donated to a named charitable institution. (Fraser Valley Regional Library and CUPE Local 1698)

Some collective agreements provide that an "arbitration board shall have the power to transfer or discipline any person found guilty of sexually harassing an employee." (City of Victoria and CUPE Local 50)

Another collective agreement provides that an "arbitration board shall have the power to transfer, discipline or levy a financial penalty against the harasser and the employer." (Municipality of Terrace (B.C.) and CUPE Local 2012)

8. *Action for frivolous complaints:*

   Collective agreements also provide that, where a complaint is determined to be of a frivolous, vindictive or vexatious nature, the employer may take appropriate action. Such action shall only be for just cause and may be grieved pursuant to the collective agreement. (Government of Manitoba and MGEA)

9. *Protection against personal harassment:*

A few collective agreements are now including protection against personal harassment. "Personal harassment by either employees or employer representatives shall be defined as: repeated, intentional, offensive comments and/or to cause personal humiliation." (South Vancouver Neighbourhood House and CUPE Local 2643)

In the absence of specific contract language prohibiting sexual or personal harassment, an arbitrator would have difficulty deciding what clause, if any, in the collective agreement had been violated.

Arbitrators need "enabling legislation" in order to find contractual violations.

Reprinted by permission of the Canadian Union of Public Employees.

CHAPTER NINE

How to Investigate?

WHY INVESTIGATE?

The first question in this chapter should perhaps be *why* rather than *how* we should investigate. The answer is because it is the employer's duty.

In one case, a human rights board of inquiry made it very clear that the employer was required to investigate a complaint of harassment. In that case, *Hinds v. Canada (Employment & Immigration Comm.)* (1988), 10 C.H.R.R. D/5683 (Cdn. Human Rights Trib.), the harassment was perpetrated by an unknown co-worker of the complainant. The main issue for the board of inquiry was whether the employer was liable for the actions of an unknown harasser. The board reviewed the provisions of the *Canadian Human Rights Act* which state that any act committed by an employee of any organization in the course of his or her employment shall be deemed to be an act committed by that organization. The only defence available to this provision is s. 65(2), which will exempt an organization if it can show that it did not consent to the discriminatory action, and that it exercised all due diligence to prevent it and to avoid its effects once it did occur.

In this case, the employer had established comprehensive anti-harassment policies and procedures, including awareness training and regular reviews of the policies and practices. In short, the employer had implemented a textbook wish list of policies and procedures to confront or avoid harassment in the workplace. However, the employer was still liable for the harassment because none of its promises had been acted upon. The employer's actual response to Hinds' complaint of harassment was virtually non-existent. No follow-up was done, no investigation performed.

The board commented on the employer's lack of response:

> In the matter before us, there was a failure to exercise any kind of diligence in this respect to mitigate the effects of the harassment. Unfortunately, CEIC's inaction did more damage since it left the impression with those concerned that this form of harassment was not even worthy of the commitment of investigative resources in the absence of any readily apparent clues. One gets

the sense that the matter was treated as though it was considered a harmless joke to which Mr. Hinds overreacted and that it would be best if the whole thing was simply forgotten. (at page D/5694)

The employer's response, which is clearly demonstrated by an investigation, is critical. It helps the employer find out what happened, address the issues, work toward restoring employee morale and avoid liability.

HOW TO RECEIVE COMPLAINTS

Once an organization acknowledges its responsibility to investigate complaints of harassment, the next question becomes "how to go about it?" The process should be outlined in the workplace harassment policy. The questions that must be addressed to flesh out the process are the remaining four classic queries — "who", "what", "where" and "when", "why" having been addressed at the beginning of this chapter.

Who?

The organization must identify individuals who are available to respond to employee questions or concerns about workplace harassment and who can receive complaints. For the balance of this chapter, these employees will be referred to as "designated employees" and the employees who complain of harassment as "complainants". The designated employees need not be the individuals who will investigate or propose resolutions for the complaint although they can also do this if they have the necessary training and support. The designated employees will be receiving the complaints in the first instance. Depending on the approach used, the complaint can then be turned over to other internal investigators or an external third party for follow-up.

Employees who are designated to receive complaints will be identified in the workplace harassment policy. They must possess three important qualities:

1. They must be sufficiently accessible to allow employees to speak to them when necessary. This requires more than one employee where an organization's workplace is spread out over several locations. This also means that the employees who are designated must be seen to be approachable and easy to talk to.
2. They must be sufficiently senior to be seen to be able to intervene on an employee's behalf if this is necessary. If an employee is complaining about the actions of a supervisor, the employee needs to

feel that the designated employee has the clout to deal with a potentially politically difficult situation.
3. They must have received some training above and beyond that given to other employees. It is unfair and unrealistic to ask employees to act in this capacity without providing them with the tools to do so. Also, they must have the support of the organization to accomplish their task. This means that they will be permitted time away from their regular work to deal with harassment issues when they arise. They will also have access to administrative support to organize meetings with other witnesses, secure meeting rooms and type reports or notes if this is necessary.

The process of selecting these individuals varies. Sometimes the human resources department of an organization may take on the bulk of this work as they have often already received the necessary training and have demonstrated the aptitude. Alternatively, some organizations ask the employees who they would feel the most comfortable with as their designated employees. Other organizations, particularly those that are unionized, have already put in place joint committees to address workplace harassment issues. This may have been the committee that drafted the harassment policy. In this scenario, the joint committee would be the appropriate group to decide who the designated employees would be.

What? Where? and When?

These three questions are addressed together. The process contemplated for addressing harassment complaints is outlined in the following chart:

C. informs D.E. about harassing behaviour. D.E.: - listens to C., - takes notes; - schedules second meeting with C.	D.E. meets with C. to ensure D.E. has all information. D.E. decides:	1. needs further investigation. D.E.: - plans investigation, or - requests third party investigator to take over. - OR - 2. matter can be addressed by: 1) helping C. to approach H. directly to inform H. that actions are unwelcome, offensive. D.E. follows up with C. - OR - 2) an informal discussion between H. and D.E.	D.E. (or external) develops interview plan, including protocol, and schedules witness interviews	D.E. (or external) prepares report documenting findings	If qualified, D.E. includes recommended resolution.

C. = Complainant
D.E. = Designated Employee
H. = Harassing Employee

The designated employee is the front line for harassment complaints and questions. Some employees will approach that person with questions or concerns about harassment and the nuances of the policy. However, the most time-consuming part of the designated employee's job will be receiving and addressing complaints. Typically, an employee will approach the designated employee to report an incident or a series of incidents involving a co-worker, supervisor, manager or another party with whom the employee comes into contact as a result of his or her work. During the course of this initial meeting the designated employee must remember that he or she is there to listen. That's all. It is not the opportunity to propose the ultimate resolution or to interrogate anyone; there will be time for a thorough investigation later if one is required. This is when the designated employee simply listens to the employee and takes some notes.

The designated employee must never forget that harassment is a deeply personal issue for everyone concerned. If an employee comes to see the designated employee to discuss harassment issues, whether it is simply a question or a complaint, the employee is often upset and angry. This initial meeting is the time that the designated employee gives to the employee to simply vent his or her anger or discuss his or her feelings and understanding of what has occurred. An interpretation of what happened is typically neither appreciated nor appropriate at this juncture.

Once the designated employee has heard the employee's story, it is often helpful to immediately schedule another meeting with the employee to discuss the matter in more detail. This will give an opportunity to follow up with the individual later when emotions are not running so high and when the designated employee has had a chance to think about the next step. Even if the complainant is composed and prepared to discuss the matter at length, the designated employee may need some time to organize his or her approach to the incident. It is best to plan this next stage before proceeding further in order to give that employee the best assistance possible.

This next meeting must be scheduled within the next 24 hours to demonstrate that the organization is taking the complaint seriously and is committed to dealing with it. It must take place at an accessible but relatively private location that will be free of interruptions.

DEVELOPING AN INVESTIGATION PLAN

After the initial meeting with the complainant, the designated employee must prepare for the second meeting. This second meeting will give the designated employee the opportunity to conduct a more in-depth interview where he or she can ensure that all the information that might be available from the complainant is obtained. The designated employee should arrange for administrative support if necessary and book a room that is relatively private and free from distractions, including interruptions.

After the second interview with the complainant, the designated employee must decide whether the matter needs to be formally investigated or whether it can be addressed immediately and directly by a low-key discussion with the other employee involved.

If the matter needs to be investigated, the designated employee will consult the process developed in conjunction with the harassment policy that determines who does the investigation. In some cases, designated employees are themselves trained to handle investigations. In other situations, an external third party is retained. After the investigator is named, the next step is to develop a plan, including what I have termed "an investigation protocol". The plan itself is quite simple. It should include:

1. A list of the people being interviewed. This is not cast in stone. As more information is obtained, the list may change.
2. An interview schedule. Don't underestimate the amount of time needed to conduct the interviews. They typically take far longer than anticipated because each response must be written down. Also, be sure to schedule in time to complete notes after the interview is over. Schedule a 15-minute catch-up break between interviews.
3. An outline of the questions that are certain to be asked. Write these down on separate sheets with each employee's name at the top. One of the easiest ways to save time while writing down an employee's response to a question is to have some of the questions written out ahead of time. Be sure to save plenty of space after each question. When you are trying to write things down quickly your handwriting becomes messier and generally takes more room.
4. An estimated time line including an anticipated completion date.
5. An investigation protocol. This protocol outlines the approach you will take with the individuals you interview and is described in more detail immediately below.

THE INVESTIGATION PROTOCOL

The protocol is simply the series of questions the designated employee will ask during the interview. Developing a solid investigation or interview protocol can be invaluable when you are going to be questioning several people about a complaint.

There are several steps in a general investigation protocol:

(1) Provide Introduction

Example: Describe who you are, what your qualifications are and why you were given this role.

(2) Summarize Purpose

Explain why you are conducting interviews.

Example: "The purpose of this interview is to gather information to resolve this matter".

(3) Explain Process

Briefly review the process for each interview. Ensure that each interviewee understands the context in which the interviews are to take place.

Example: "I am conducting several interviews today with people who might be able to provide some information about this".

(4) Outline Expectations

Explain that information gathering is all you are doing. Also, let people know that they may well have nothing to add. In such a case, you don't expect them to offer anything.

Example: "We conduct these interviews to get an accurate account of the conflict and to find a means to resolve the problem. We don't expect that each person will be able to find us all the information we need. Only answer the questions you feel you can."

(5) Stress Confidentiality

Don't ever guarantee confidentiality. It is not possible to maintain complete confidentiality in most investigations. Often, the subject matter will be disclosed in other interviews, including the interview with the alleged harasser. Or the information you receive frequently engenders further questions in subsequent interviews. In investigations, it is important to determine if a pattern exists — have other employees ever witnessed similar instances, been subjected to similar behaviour?

On many occasions, the subject matter will be recorded in written records which could be disclosed in subsequent litigation if it occurs. Alternatively, documents could be disclosed to an employee under Freedom of Information legislation if the employer is a public body and the legislation is in place in the jurisdiction.

However, you can provide the individual with some comfort that the information he or she divulges will not be a subject of general discussion. Also, it helps to underscore the seriousness of the interview.

Example: "The information we will discuss today is in strict confidence. It will only ever be disclosed to the extent necessary to resolve this matter."

(6) Make General Statements

General statements will help avoid the disclosure of confidential information to some extent. They also help to provide some focus to the discussion without narrowing the field with the assumption that the particular behaviour complained of is the only occurrence. It can also help avoid naming any individuals at the beginning of the interview.

Example: "Your supervisor is concerned about allegations of harassment involving some of the employees."

(7) Ask Preplanned Questions

You will likely want to record the responses to your questions. Make your notes verbatim as much as possible. Paraphrasing someone's responses involves the use of assumptions. You may change their meaning unintentionally.

To enable you to have sufficient time to record the responses it helps to have the questions already written out. Leave adequate space for both the responses and for additional questions. However, for the most part, if you have reviewed the case adequately, you will know the questions that you will need to ask before you begin the interview.

Example: "What can you tell me about this?"

(8) Use Probes

Follow up on the information you are given. It is often more effective to do this generally with an open-ended question or a probe. This also helps to avoid the assumption that the individual whom you are interviewing has exhausted his or her knowledge on the topic. It also precludes any value judgments or leading questions if you can keep your follow up general.

Example: "Can you tell me more about that?"

(9) Use a Cautionary Close

Finally, after the prepared questions have been answered and all other leads have been pursued, begin to bring the interview to a close in a way that still allows for further pertinent discussion if necessary. The most relevant information you receive may not result from any of the preplanned questions. Make sure the interviewee has an opportunity to provide you with relevant information that has not been covered.

Example: "Is there anyone else I should talk to? Is there anything else you feel I should know about this?"

DOCUMENTING THE FINDINGS

Harassment investigation findings are generally documented in a report. Some reports include recommendations for resolution of the complaint, for the complainant and possibly for the person about whom it was made. This recommendation must be made by an individual who understands the potential ramifications of a wrongful dismissal or other consequence.

Generally, a report can include the following information:

(a) Background

The background information in a harassment investigation report includes:

- name of complainant(s)
- date complaint made to employer representative
- date alleged incidents occurred
- general nature of complaint (sexual, racial, etc.)
- name of alleged harasser(s)
- specific allegations
- who was interviewed and when
- materials reviewed, if any.

(b) Findings

Based on the information obtained, some decisions must be made. Obviously, these decisions must be made with a great degree of care. Look for completeness of facts and carefully examine the totality of the circumstances. Information included under "Findings" should include:

(i) whether the alleged behaviour occurred;
(ii) whether the behaviour was harassment. Look to the definition of harassment in the policy. Does it fit what happened?
(iii) other factors that should be considered, such as:

- severity of harassment
- frequency of harassment

- time span
- injury incurred, if any
- type of evidence
- position of complainant
- position and length of service of alleged harasser
- effect on the workplace
- previous warnings.

(c) Recommendations

The section on recommendations covers corrective action that can address the needs of the complainant.

In addition, if harassment was found to have taken place, the report should present options for discipline in the recommendations section. Possibilities include:

- education
- training
- counselling
- warning
- transfer
- demotion
- suspension
- discharge
- re-issue policy.

(d) Appendices

Some reports include appendices in which additional material is attached. One of the most common examples is an appendix with interview notes or the original written complaint.

CHAPTER TEN

What Do the Human Rights Commissions Say?

PUBLICATIONS

Several human rights commissions across Canada have published helpful material on workplace harassment. Most of it deals with sexual harassment as this represents the most common complaint received by many of the commissions. Some, like Alberta, have prepared sample sexual harassment policies for employers. It has been reproduced in Chapter Eight. Some focus on other types of harassment. Each of these publications is reprinted below to help organizations in each jurisdiction discover what their own commission has to say on the topic.

CANADIAN HUMAN RIGHTS COMMISSION

HARASSMENT

The *Canadian Human Rights Act* contains the following prohibition against harassment:

s. 14.1 (1) It is a discriminatory practice,

   (*a*) in the provision of goods, services, facilities or accommodation customarily available to the general public.
   (*b*) in the provision of commercial premises or residential accommodation, or
   (*c*) in matters related to employment,

to harass an individual on a prohibited ground of discrimination.

(2) Without limiting the generality of sub-section (1), sexual harassment shall, for the purposes of that subsection, be deemed to be harassment on a prohibited ground of discrimination. 1980-81-82-83, c. 143, s. 7.

Commission Policy

- protection against acts of harassment extends to incidents occurring at or away from the workplace, during or outside normal working hours provided such acts are committed within the course of employment, or in the provision of goods, services, facilities or accommodation;
- harassment may be related to any of the discriminatory grounds contained in the *Canadian Human Rights Act*. Such behaviour may be verbal, physical, deliberate, unsolicited or unwelcome; it may be one incident or a series of incidents. While the following is not an exhaustive list, harassment may include:

    - verbal abuse or threats;
    - unwelcome remarks, jokes, innuendos or taunting about a person's body, attire, age, marital status, ethnic or national origin, religion, etc;
    - displaying of pornographic, racist or other offensive or derogatory pictures;
    - practical jokes which cause awkwardness or embarrassment;
    - unwelcome invitations or requests, whether indirect or explicit, or intimidation;
    - leering or other gestures;
    - condescension or paternalism which undermines self-respect;
    - unnecessary physical contact such as touching, patting, pinching, punching;
    - physical assault;

- for a practice to be considered harassment it must be reasonably perceived as a term or condition of employment (including availability or continuation of work, promotional or training opportunities) or of the provision of goods, services, facilities or accommodation customarily available to the general public; or influence decisions on such matters; or interfere with job performance or access to or enjoyment of goods, services, facilities or accommodation; or humiliate, insult or intimidate any individual;
- any act of harassment committed by an employee or an agent of any employer in the course of the employment shall be considered to be an act committed by that employer;
- an act of harassment shall not, however, be considered to be an act committed by an employer if it is established that the employer did not consent to the commission of the act and exercised all due diligence to prevent the act from being committed and, subsequently, to mitigate or avoid its consequences;

- harassment will be considered to have taken place if a reasonable person ought to have known that such behaviour was unwelcome;
- in investigating and deciding each case, there must be an objective examination of all the circumstances (including the nature and context of the incidents).

Reproduced with permission of the Minister of Public Works and Government Services, 1995.

ALBERTA HUMAN RIGHTS COMMISSION

DEVELOPING AND CREATING AN EFFECTIVE SEXUAL HARASSMENT POLICY

Developing an effective workplace policy is key in preventing sexual harassment. Education is also important. People have to **know** there is a policy and what it says. The employer's position on sexual harassment should be contained in a clear policy statement, distributed to all employees, posted on bulletin boards and provided to all managers, supervisors and new employees.

Leadership is critical to any effective sexual harassment policy. With a well developed policy, senior management has a chance to demonstrate a proud corporate commitment to fair and equal treatment, regardless of gender.

Managers should take a lead role in reminding staff (in newsletters, annual reports, at meetings, etc.) that sexual harassment is against company policy **and** the law.

Policies that work do these things:

- **Encourage employees** to come forward with complaints. How a policy sounds and is structured is important. Management has to demonstrate its commitment to eliminating sexual harassment.
- **Ensure acceptance** by all staff. This can only be developed through consultation, input and feedback. <u>Time taken here will be more than repaid down the road.</u>
- **Provide a clear definition** of sexual harassment, as outlined in the *Individual's Rights Protection Act*.
- **Include guidelines** for individuals seeking advice about filing a sexual harassment complaint.
- **Stress confidentiality** of complaints and assure employees they will be protected from retaliation.
- **Designate a person or persons** to hear complaints. These individual(s) should be viewed by other employees as neutral but as

having the authority to act. If possible, have more than one person delegated to this important, sometimes emotionally-taxing job.
- **Lay out the steps**: effective sexual harassment policies provide a step-by-step description of what happens in your company when a claim of sexual harassment is investigated. To encourage prevention, also spell out the disciplinary consequences of harassment of any employee.
- **Guarantee a fair and prompt reaction** to anyone with a complaint of sexual harassment.

(See Commission Fact Sheet titled Sample Sexual Harassment Policy)

Education and Prevention

Education is important in preventing sexual harassment. Everyone must know about the policy and management must remind staff at all levels, on an ongoing basis, of its commitment to it. A sensitive policy can serve to foster an understanding of the true nature of sexual harassment and its destructive consequences. Remember: prevention is better than cure, and prevention should provide the basis of a sexual harassment policy.

Reprinted by permission of the Alberta Human Rights Commission.

SEXUAL HARASSMENT

What is Sexual Harassment?

Any unwelcome behaviour, sexual in nature, that adversely affects, or threatens to affect, directly or indirectly, a person's job security, working conditions or prospects for promotion or earnings; or prevents a person from getting a job, living accommodations or any kind of public service.

Sexual harassment is usually an attempt by one person to use their "perceived power"— their position of authority — over someone else.

Sexual harassment is discrimination on the ground of gender and is prohibited in Alberta's *Individual's Rights Protection Act* and under every other human rights legislation in Canada.

Sexual harassment violations are among the most frequent complaints received by human rights agencies, and the most costly for employers who fail to treat such complaints seriously.

Who is Most Affected?

Men are sometimes sexually harassed by women and same-gender harassment does happen. However, surveys show that roughly 70 percent of women versus 15 percent of men are victims of sexual harassment in the workplace.

What Constitutes Sexual Harassment?

It can be expressed in many ways, (from very subtle to most obvious) through any of the following:

- suggestive remarks or compromising invitations
- verbal abuse
- display of suggestive images
- leering or whistling
- patting, rubbing or other unwanted physical contact
- outright demands for sexual favours
- physical assault.

Sexual Harassment and Workplace Romance

<u>Mutually acceptable workplace flirtation is not sexual harassment.</u> Sexual harassment is unwanted, often coercive, sexual behaviour directed by one person toward another. It is emotionally abusive and creates an unhealthy atmosphere in the workplace.

Who is Legally Responsible?

The Supreme Court of Canada has decided that in cases of proven sexual harassment employers are responsible for the actions of their employees.

Lack of awareness by management does not necessarily eliminate this liability.

Employer Responsibilities

In Alberta, employers are responsible for maintaining a work environment free from sexual harassment for all employees, customers and clients.

A supervisor who neglects to follow up on a complaint of sexual harassment may be liable under the *Individual's Rights Protection Act* for failing to take prompt and appropriate action.

Not having an effective policy on sexual harassment in place can increase an employer's liability in the event of a complaint being filed. Prompt and appropriate action on sexual harassment complaints can reduce employer liability still further.

Sexual Harassment Policy Development

Commission staff are available to consult with employers on the development of policies to deal with sexual harassment in the workplace.

Seminars are provided on request, free of charge, to help management and employees understand the rights and responsibilities behind any effective policy against sexual harassment.

What Can a Victim Do?

Anyone who believes he or she has been sexually harassed should first make it clear to the offender and/or to a person in authority that such action is unwanted.

If the behaviour persists, or corrective action is not taken, a complaint may be filed with the Alberta Human Rights Commission. This must be done within *six months* of the alleged incident, or the Commission does not have the authority to investigate.

For the purposes of later investigation, a record should be kept of when the alleged incidents occurred, the nature of the behaviour, the names of any witnesses and any other information useful to the investigation.

Note: A complaint must be filed with the Alberta Human Rights Commission within six months of the alleged incident.

Reprinted by permission of the Alberta Human Rights Commission.

BRITISH COLUMBIA HUMAN RIGHTS COMMISSION

SEXUAL HARASSMENT AND HUMAN RIGHTS

This pamphlet is about sexual harassment, and the protections against it that are available under the British Columbia *Human Rights Act*.

It explains:

- what the law says about sexual harassment
- how you can file a sexual harassment complaint with the Human Rights Council
- where you can get more information.

What is sexual harassment?

Sexual harassment is "unwelcome conduct of a sexual nature" that has a negative effect on where you work, or live, or receive services. It can be verbal or physical. "Unwelcome" attention includes any attention that a reasonable person would know is unwanted or unwelcome. Sexual harassment often occurs in a situation where the harasser has more power than you do.

What are some examples of sexual harassment?

Some examples of sexual harassment include:

- verbal abuse or threats
- unwelcome remarks, jokes, innuendoes or taunting
- displaying of pornographic or other offensive pictures
- practical jokes that cause awkwardness or embarrassment
- unwelcome invitations or requests
- leering or other gestures
- unnecessary physical contact such as touching, patting, pinching, punching
- sexual assault (this may also be a criminal matter)

Sexual harassment can include negative comments that are gender based. Comments such as "fat cow" and "waddles like a duck" and "women should go back home where they belong" have been considered sexual harassment.

Sexual harassment usually involves women who have been harassed by men. However, there are cases where men have been sexually harassed.

Mr. A gave his secretary unwanted gifts and wrote her unwanted letters of affection. He phoned her at home at night and made sexually suggestive remarks.

Ms. B worked in a video store. One of her co-workers regularly tried to get her to look at pornographic pictures.

Ms. C's landlord began showing up at her place at night. He would ask questions such as "Aren't you lonely without a man about the house?" and make explicit sexual remarks.

Mr. D, a professor, invited one of his women students to his home. She thought a number of students would be there, but they were alone. She had to fend off his attempts to hug and kiss her.

SEXUAL HARASSMENT IN THE WORKPLACE

Sexual harassment in the workplace may include a promise of reward in exchange for sexual favours. Or it may include a threat, either stated or unstated, that if you don't go along with the harassment there will be job consequences. Consequences can include losing your job, or not getting the shift you want, or being demoted, or being denied a promotion.

Sexual harassment can also occur without any promises of reward, or threats. The harassment can make the workplace an intimidating, hostile, or offensive place. This is sometimes called "a poisoned work environment."

What does the law say about sexual harassment?

Sexual harassment is discrimination on the basis of sex. The law says that employers have a duty to provide a healthy and respectful work environment free from sexual harassment. If harassment occurs in the workplace, employers are responsible. Employers have been held liable for harassment of employees by their supervisors, co-workers, or clients.

Harassing actions need not be intentional in order to be considered sexual harassment. "It was just a joke," or "I meant it as a compliment" is no excuse under the law.

What can I do about sexual harassment?

If you are being sexually harassed it's a good idea to think about what action you can take. Keep in mind that the harassment is not your fault. Harassers are responsible for their own behaviour. Always remember this when you take any action to stop sexual harassment.

Here are some things you can do:

Keep a record

It's very important to keep a written record of the harassment. Keep track of times and dates, and witnesses, if any. Witnesses may include people who saw the harassment, and people you spoke to about the harassment. Write down exactly what each of you said, and how the harassment made you feel, physically and emotionally. If you have received any letters from the harasser, keep them. This information will be vital, especially if you file a human rights complaint.

Talk about the harassment

Talk to your fellow employees, or other tenants or students. This may be difficult, especially at first, but it can be very helpful to you. If others saw the harassment, tell them that you are thinking about taking action. If nobody saw the harassment, tell other people about it. Describe what happened and how you feel.

People who know about the harassment may be witnesses for you when you take action. Also, the harasser may be harassing others as well.

Let the harasser know what you think

If you can, it's a good idea to let the harasser know the behaviour is unwelcome. You may be able to do this by consistently ignoring suggestive comments and gestures.

Or you may tell the harasser directly what you think of the behaviour. You can do this in person or in writing. If you confront the harasser in person, take someone with you as a witness and for support.

Report the harassment

Report the harassment to your supervisor, or the harasser's supervisor, other senior management personnel or faculty. It's a good idea to complain as soon as you feel able to. Sometimes people see long delays as a sign that you aren't taking the harassment seriously.

Get help from the community

Get some support from a local women's group or community group. There are groups who have experience in helping people deal with sexual harassment. They may help you figure out which option to take, and give you emotional support.

If you need legal advice about what to do, you may want to contact your local Legal Services Society office.

Taking action to end sexual harassment can be complicated because you live in a small community, or because English is not your first language. Contact your nearest women's centre, aboriginal organization or immigrant-serving agency for support.

What legal options do I have?

You have a number of legal options. You can choose one or more of these options. For example, you can use the company's internal complaint procedure and also file a human rights complaint.

Your options include the following:

Use an internal complaint procedure

If your company or school or university has a policy against sexual harassment, check it to see if it has a complaint procedure. If there is no complaint procedure, you may want to ask the personnel manager or student counsellor what steps to take.

Use the union procedure

Talk to your shop steward about how the union deals with sexual harassment. The collective agreement may have a sexual harassment or sex discrimination clause.

File a complaint with British Columbia Council of Human Rights

Phone or write the British Columbia Council of Human Rights. A human rights officer will tell you if you have grounds for a complaint under the *Human Rights Act*. The officer will assist you with the necessary forms.

You need to file a complaint *within 6 months* of the discrimination. In special cases, the Council may extend this time limit.

Services provided by the Council are free.

How long can the process take?

If your complaint goes all the way to a hearing, it can take up to two years. If a settlement is reached before a hearing, it will not take as long.

What happens when I file a complaint?

Sometimes the Council can help you settle a complaint without having to go through the formal complaint process. The officer can contact the person you are making the complaint about and try to mediate an agreement that you are both happy with. The officer will not do this without your permission.

If you cannot reach an agreement, the Council will assign an investigator to your case.

What will the investigator do?

The investigator will meet separately with you, with the person you complained about, and with any witnesses either of you think might help explain what happened. If you and the person you complained about both agree, you may meet together with the investigator.

The investigator then prepares a report for the Council. Both you and the person you are complaining about get a copy of the report. You can give more information to the Council *up to 30 days* after you receive the report.

What happens next?

Based on the investigator's report, the Council will decide either to hold a hearing or dismiss your complaint. If there is a hearing, you will be told the date, time and place. You can contact a lawyer to act for you at the hearing. Legal aid will be available to you (look in the white pages of the phone book under "Legal Aid").

What happens after a decision is made?

After the hearing, the Council member makes a decision and gives reasons in writing. If you disagree with the decision, you can ask the British Columbia Supreme Court to review the decision. You cannot appeal this decision through the Council.

If the Council decides that you have been discriminated against because of sexual harassment, the Council will make an order prohibiting further discrimination against you or other people.

In addition, the Council may also order that you get:

- your job back, or the promotion you were going for, or whatever else you lost by being discriminated against
- money for wages you may have lost or money that you may have lost because of the discrimination
- money for damages to your feelings.

Mr. F, the company president, repeatedly made sexually suggestive remarks about Ms. G, the office manager. He commented on her appearance and her body, and invited her to have sexual intercourse with him. These sexually explicit remarks were often made in front of other staff members and customers. Mr. F. fired Ms. G on the grounds that she was "curt, rude and feisty" in her response to him.

The Council found that Ms. G lost her job because she refused to accept sexual harassment as a condition of her employment. The Council ordered the employer to pay $24,000 as compensation for wages lost due to the discrimination, and $2000 as compensation for the humiliation Ms. G had suffered.

Can anyone do anything to me if I file a human rights complaint?

No. You, and your witnesses are protected by law from any retaliation once you have laid a human rights complaint. Your employer cannot fire or suspend you, and your landlord cannot evict you. They cannot harass you or intimidate you. If they do, you can file a separate human rights complaint.

Reprinted by permission of the British Columbia Human Rights Commission.

MANITOBA HUMAN RIGHTS COMMISSION

FACT SHEET: PROHIBITING HARASSMENT

Everyone has the right to equality of opportunity. Individuals are sometimes denied equality when they are subjected to harassment because of a group to which they belong. *The Manitoba Human Rights Code* prohibits harassment in employment, housing accommodation and the provision of services or contracts. Employers, landlords and service providers are not only legally responsible for their own acts of harassment, but may also become liable for such conduct by their employees, tenants or clients. The onus is on management to take reasonable steps to prevent harassment.

What is Harassment?

Harassment [*The Manitoba Human Rights Code*, S. 19(2)], is *a course of abusive and unwelcome conduct or comment* that is directed at individuals because of a group to which they belong or appear to belong.

Different groups can be the target of harassment. Racial harassment, for example, can include racial slurs or name calling directed at a person or persons of native ancestry or of a visible minority. Repeated remarks to a female employee that she should be at home raising her children could be harassment based on sex and family status.

Harassment can occur in a variety of settings: in the workplace against employees, in the provision of housing against tenants, or in the provision of services against customers or clients. Inaction by management which is aware, or ought to be aware of harassment, could result in a human rights complaint.

Harassment can also be a *series of objectionable and unwelcome sexual solicitations or advances*. Sexual harassment can also occur in the employment setting or in the provision of housing or services. It would be a contravention of *The Code*, for example, if a landlord made repeated and unwanted sexually suggestive remarks to a tenant, or if an employer threatened to terminate an employee for not complying with sexual demands.

Why Should You Act?

Employers, landlords and service providers are legally obligated to take reasonable steps to provide an environment free from harassment. Failure to do so can result in:

- a poisoned business environment
- loss of productivity and business
- high rate of staff or tenant turnover
- a human rights complaint
- payment of monetary compensation if the complaint is substantiated
- damage to your reputation

What Should You Do?

Any employer, landlord or service provider should take active steps to discourage harassment in the workplace, and must do so if they are aware, or ought to be aware, that harassment is occurring in their place of business.

Take all reasonable steps to prevent harassment...to terminate harassment once it has occurred ... to mitigate or avoid the effect of harassment.

Such reasonable steps may include:

- developing internal policies to deal with harassment
- communicating these policies to all employees
- informing the harasser that the behaviour will not be tolerated and that disciplinary action or dismissal may follow if the behaviour continues
- taking disciplinary action where appropriate
- providing protection and support for the victim
- contacting The Manitoba Human Rights Commission for assistance.

Know your *Code*!

Human rights legislation has paramount status in Manitoba. This means that where there is a conflict with other provincial legislation, the *Human Rights Code* prevails.

This information is a simplified description of provisions under the *Human Rights Code*. For more information, consult *The Code* or contact The Manitoba Human Rights Commission.

Prepared by the Manitoba Human Rights Commission (effective April 18, 1988) and reprinted with its permission.

NEW BRUNSWICK HUMAN RIGHTS COMMISSION

SEXUAL HARASSMENT IN EMPLOYMENT

Mary's boss often asks her to join him for a drink to "discuss her career". He keeps saying that he "could really help her if she was little friendlier."

Susan works with five men who often make remarks such as "This is a man's job" or "Women should be home doing dishes and washing." Sometimes they brush up against her, grab her or pinch her.

Mary and Susan are being sexually harassed.

What is sexual harassment on the job?

Sexual actions, comments or requests in the course of employment are sexual harassment if they are unwelcome or if decisions affecting employees or job applicants are based on submission to or rejection of such conduct.

Sexual harassment directed at men or women is illegal, even if it is only a single incident. In addition to conduct occurring in the regular course of employment, sexual harassment includes conduct occurring off the job site or outside working hours, provided employment decisions are based on submission to such harassment.

Sexual conduct is not sexual harassment if it is consensual. However, consent is not valid if it is obtained through threats or promises concerning employment. Also, silence does not necessarily mean consent; a harasser will be liable if he or she ought reasonably to have known that the behaviour was unwelcome.

Examples of sexual harassment include:

- degrading remarks about either sex;
- unwelcome pinching, hugging, brushing up against and patting;
- unwelcome sexual requests, remarks, jokes or gestures;
- unfair evaluations or reprimands, reduced working hours, overwork, dismissals, discipline or refusals to hire, when they are in retaliation for refusing to submit to sexual harassment.

Are employers responsible for preventing sexual harassment?

Yes. An employer who has not taken appropriate steps to prevent sexual harassment is liable for harassment by managers and other employees, even if the employer was unaware of the harassment. In certain cases, employers may also be liable when employees harass customers or are harassed by them. Accordingly, it is important for employers to develop policies and procedures on sexual harassment.

Why is it good business for employers to prevent sexual harassment?

Sexual harassment may result in stress, increased sick leave, low morale, low productivity and high turnover. Complaints of sexual harassment can also consume a great deal of time and lead to negative publicity and major legal expenses.

How can employers prevent sexual harassment?

- Develop a sexual harassment policy that establishes a procedure for investigating complaints quickly, confidentially and impartially. It should ensure that action is taken against harassers and that victims are protected from reprisals.

- Post the sexual harassment policy and ensure that all employees are aware of it.
- Take action to eliminate sexist jokes.
- Remove sexist or indecent posters, graffiti and photos.
- Provide training on sexual harassment for managers and employees; emphasize the seriousness of the issue.

What should I do if I am sexually harassed?

- Do not ignore the harassment; it will probably get worse if you do.
- Tell the harasser that the behaviour is unwelcome, either verbally or in writing.

If the harassment persists,

- Contact the Human Rights Commission for advice or to file a complaint.
- Record the details of every incident, including time, date, witnesses, exactly what each of you said and how it made you feel physically and emotionally.
- If possible, get support from employees and former employees who may have been witnesses or may have been harassed themselves.
- Avoid being alone with the harasser if possible.

How can the N.B. Human Rights Commission help me if I have been harassed?

The Commission can give you advice about the various options that are available. You do not need to give your name just to get advice.

If you were harassed within the last year, you may file a complaint with the Human Rights Commission. The employer and harasser will be informed of the complaint. A Human Rights Officer will investigate it and, if the evidence supports the complaint, will attempt to negotiate a voluntary settlement. This service is free of charge.

If the employer does not offer a fair settlement, a Board of Inquiry may be appointed to hold a public hearing. If the Board upholds the complaint, it may order the employer to rehire you or to compensate you for loss of pay, for example.

It is illegal for the employer to fire you because you filed a formal complaint. You do not need to file complaint under the employer's sexual harassment policy, or quit your job, before filing a complaint with the Commission.

Apart from filing a human rights complaint, what else can I do?

You may be able to file a complaint under the employer's sexual harassment policy, file a grievance with the union or start a lawsuit through a lawyer.

An intentional, non-consensual physical contact, or a threat or attempt to do so, is a criminal assault and should be reported to the police.

What about other types of harassment?

In addition to sexual harassment, the *Human Rights Act* prohibits harassment based on race, sexual orientation, national origin, disability, religion, or any of the other grounds listed in the Act.

The Act applies not only to employment, but also to housing, public services and certain associations. They also must be free of harassment.

Reprinted by permission of the New Brunswick Human Rights Commission.

NEWFOUNDLAND HUMAN RIGHTS COMMISSION

SEXUAL HARASSMENT IN THE WORKPLACE

Sexual harassment can occur to any person regardless of his/her age, occupation, physical appearance or marital status. It is not a new phenomenon. People have been the victims of sexual harassment for years, but until recently the problem was not taken seriously. Now, along with an increasing awareness of the extent of sexual harassment, there is concern about developing strategies to deal with it.

There are steps that employees and employers can take when faced with the problem and we have outlined these here. Sexual harassment is prohibited under section 13 of the *Human Rights Code*.

Sexual Harassment: A Definition

A sexual solicitation or advance made by an employer or other person who is in a position to confer, grant or deny a benefit or advancement when the person making the solicitation or advance knows or ought reasonably to know that it is unwelcome. A complaint can be made against a co-worker where a supervisor has been advised of the matter.

No person in a position to confer or deny a benefit or advancement shall penalize, punish, or threaten reprisal against that person for the rejection of a sexual solicitation or advance.

As an employee:

Your rights

If you believe you are a victim of sexual harassment as described in the foregoing definition, you should contact the office of the Human Rights

Commission and explain that you wish to lay a complaint of sexual harassment under the *Human Rights Code*.

The Human Rights Commission will examine your complaint after obtaining all the information from you.

If the opinion is reached that there should be further investigation and that possibly a Board of Inquiry should be appointed, the Human Rights Commission will proceed to do this.

And what you should do:

1. Make it clear to the harasser that the conduct is unwelcome and unacceptable.
2. Document each case of sexual harassment i.e. time, date, place, person involved, description of the type of harassment, any witnesses. If there are witnesses, have them sign your documentation.
3. Check with co-workers to see if they have experienced similar harassment and document these cases.
4. Report all cases of sexual harassment to a person in a position of authority.
5. Use the legal protection available. Before you decide to leave your job because of sexual harassment, report the case to the Human Rights Commission and obtain advice on the proper action to take.
6. Remember, you do not have to tolerate sexual harassment. Say "no" firmly and indicate you will not be intimidated and that you will take whatever action is necessary to protect your rights.

DON'T FEEL GUILTY: IN SEXUAL HARASSMENT CASES, IT IS THE HARASSER WHO IS WRONG — NOT THE VICTIM!!

As an employer:

Your responsibility

As an employer you should know that if you are aware of any civil misbehaviour of your employees, you may be held accountable. If one of your employees is successfully charged with sexual harassment against a person under his/her supervision, under the *Human Rights Code*, you as the employer can be made a party to that complaint.

And what you can do:

1. Send out a letter defining sexual harassment and your policy on it, to all staff and post it on employee bulletin boards.
2. Discuss sexual harassment in management and supervisory training sessions. Make supervisory personnel aware of the repercussions of sexual harassment and what it means to the work environment.

3. In orientation sessions with new employees, deal with the issue of sexual harassment and make it known that you will treat any complaints seriously.
4. Ensure that parties to complaints of sexual harassment are protected from reprisals from each other, or other workers, during the investigative process.

Reprinted by permission of the Newfoundland Human Rights Commission.

NOVA SCOTIA HUMAN RIGHTS COMMISSION

WHAT IS SEXUAL HARASSMENT?

Every Nova Scotian should be able to go to work, belong to an association or have access to public services without being sexually harassed. The *Human Rights Act* has made sexual harassment illegal in all areas of public life.

If someone makes sexual advances towards you, requests sexual favours in exchange for a benefit, make sexual comments or physically touches you in a sexual manner, you could be experiencing sexual harassment.

Most sexual harassment complaints are filed by women against men but complaints are also taken from men who allege harassment by women or between individuals of the same sex.

Sexual harassment occurs when the harasser knows or ought to know that the behaviour is offensive and unwelcome.

Sexual harassment can take many forms and is not restricted to the following:

- Displaying pictures or objects of a sexual nature
- Staring, leering
- Gestures
- Commenting on a person's appearance, attire or anatomy
- Unwelcome invitations or requests of a sexual nature
- Physical touching, patting or pinching
- Unwelcome remarks, jokes, innuendoes or comments of a sexual nature.

Statistics show that sexual harassment is a serious problem which affects society as a whole. Using the workplace as an example, consider the implications sexual harassment has for those involved.

- The employee being harassed may experience physical and mental health problems.

- On-the-job harassment means poor work performance and strained relations with other co-workers.
- The stress of experiencing sexual harassment has a personal effect on life after work hours as well.
- Relationships with family members and friends may suffer.
- Companies are also concerned about sexual harassment because sexual harassment complaints affect their reputations in the community, result in staff turnover, and productivity lessens.
- Even if a company has a sexual harassment policy in place liability for the acts of its employees may still result.
- Although the workplace is used as an example, sexual harassment is prohibited in all areas of public life and this includes the provision of accommodation, services, and facilities.

Sexual harassment can be prevented if we treat one another with dignity and respect. We must all share responsibility in the fight against sexual harassment. The Nova Scotia Human Rights Commission offers assistance against harassment in a number of ways:

- We will investigate complaints.
- We provide awareness/educational sessions on sexual harassment.
- We will advise on the drafting of policies on sexual harassment.
- Persons who believe they are being harassed are invited to contact the Human Rights Commission for advice and information even before filing a complaint.

Reprinted by permission of the Nova Scotia Human Rights Commission.

COMMUNITY LEGAL INFORMATION ASSOCIATION OF P.E.I. INC.

SEXUAL HARASSMENT

Julia is feeling more and more uncomfortable with her co-worker Brian. In the firm in which they work, she and Brian have to work together developing funding proposals and carrying out projects. The problem is that Brian is always asking questions about her personal life and often makes teasing remarks of a sexual nature. When she tries to discourage him, he makes their teamwork very difficult, often not keeping her informed and making her appear incompetent in front of their clients.

Is this Sexual Harassment?

Yes it is. Sexual harassment is a discriminatory practice under the *Canada Labour Code*, the *Canadian Human Rights Act*, the *Prince Edward Island*

Human Rights Act and the *Employment Standards Act* of Prince Edward Island.

All of these Acts give you the right to employment free of sexual harassment. The responsibility lies with the employer to see that it does not happen, and to take appropriate steps if it is reported.

Sexual harassment is gender (or sex) based discrimination. Although it can happen to men, it happens primarily to women and it happens because they are women.

There are two categories of sexual harassment:

- inappropriate sexual requirements from your supervisor or employer;
- a destructive work environment where the conditions of employment include unwanted sexual advances, unwanted requests for sexual favours, and other unwanted verbal, written or physical behaviour of a sexual nature.

Some examples of harassment are:

- questions and discussions about sexual activities, suggestive remarks and innuendos, bragging about sexual prowess, and proposals of physical intimacy;
- being judged on physical attributes rather than skills;
- display of pornographic or sexually degrading material;
- practical jokes of a sexual nature which cause awkwardness or embarrassment;
- letters and notes expressing sexual intentions;
- leering or other gestures;
- unnecessary physical contact.

Sexual harassment is not sexual joking, flirtation and discussions of a sexual nature between two or more EQUALLY CONSENTING adults.

Sexual harassment is a major source of anxiety for many women and some men and can cause them severe problems with their health as well as threatening their jobs and future career plans.

What can Julia do?

Julia does not have to put up with this behaviour. She can inform her employer and if nothing is done to stop the harassment she can take her case to the Human Rights Commission. Julia should keep notes on every act of harassment that occurs, including a description of the act, times, dates, and witnesses.

What will the Commission do?

They will listen to Julia and they will investigate. The Commission will talk to Julia's employer, Brian and any witnesses. If they reach the opinion that yes, there was sexual harassment, they will try to negotiate a settlement between Julia and her employer that is agreeable to both.

If an agreement cannot be reached a Human Rights Hearing will be held. At this point Julia may want to talk to a lawyer. The Commission's services are free and confidentiality is assured. However, once a public hearing is held the information becomes public and the hearings are open to media and the public.

Many places of employment have a sexual harassment policy in place. They state very clearly what to do if you are being harassed in this way.

- Don't ignore it, it won't go away, probably it will just get worse.
- Understand that you do not have to put up with it.
- Inform the harasser. If the behaviour doesn't stop, inform your supervisor, union representative, or other appropriate person on staff.
- If nothing happens file a complaint with the Human Rights Commission or follow the other steps outlined in your workplace policy.
- Keep notes of every act of harassment with times, dates, description, and names of witnesses. This is VERY IMPORTANT.
- Finally share the information with your co-workers. Other workers may have been harassed too.

Reprinted by permission of the Community
Legal Information Association of P.E.I. Inc.

SASKATCHEWAN HUMAN RIGHTS COMMISSION

SEXUAL HARASSMENT

The Saskatchewan Human Rights Code

Promoting and protecting individual dignity and equal rights — that's the goal of *The Saskatchewan Human Rights Code*. It's the Saskatchewan Human Rights Commission's job to administer the *Code* to discourage and eliminate discrimination against everyone under provincial jurisdiction — in schools, housing, public services, contracts, publications, and on the job.

Under the *Code*, it is illegal to discriminate against anyone in those protected areas because of race, religion, creed, sex, marital status, disability, colour, nationality, ancestry, place of origin, age (18-64), family status, sexual orientation or receipt of public assistance. Individuals, private companies, school boards, trade unions, professional associations — as well as provincial and municipal governments — are subject to human rights laws. Anyone who violates the *Code* could be liable for damages that result from discrimination.

What is Sexual Harassment?

Sexual harassment is a form of discrimination that's against the law.

It's any unwanted sexual conduct that interferes with rights guaranteed by *The Saskatchewan Human Rights Code*. Sexual harassment is not allowed in the workplace, at schools or universities, or in the provision of a public service. Customers in a restaurant, for example, or patients seeking medical attention, or tenants renting an apartment are protected against sexual harassment.

Sexual harassment may be verbal, physical or visual. It may be one incident or a series of incidents. It is always unsolicited and unwelcome behaviour, and can take many forms, including, but not limited to:

- sexual remarks
- "jokes" with sexual overtones
- a sexual advance or invitation
- displaying offensive pictures or photographs
- threats
- leering
- physical contact like touching, patting, pinching or brushing against
- sexual or physical assault

A Power Play

Sexual harassment is an expression of power. It may be accompanied by threats, promises or abuse.

Most sexual harassment occurs in the workplace. The harasser (most often a man) is usually someone in authority who uses his power to intimidate another (usually a woman). The victim often hesitates to complain for fear of reprisals or economic consequences.

The *Code*'s provisions against sexual harassment do not rule out office romance, flirtation or good-natured jesting that is accepted by both parties. Sexual harassment refers only to unwelcome behaviour, which the harasser knew, or should have known, would be unwanted.

Sexual Harassment ...Who Says?

Men and women have different perceptions of sexual harassment. What may be a lighthearted joke to many men may be offensive to many women.

In fact, the courts have said that women are more adversely affected by sexual harassment than men. Because of the disparity in interpretation and the fact that sexual harassment affects men and women differently, it's critical to interpret sexual harassment as any behaviour the *victim* perceives as offensive.

How Does the Victim Feel?

Victims of sexual harassment feel humiliated, ashamed, degraded, embarrassed, and angry.

Sexual harassment impairs job performance, decreases job satisfaction, and causes headaches, nervousness, insomnia and anxiety attacks.

It's also wasteful. When employees have to spend time and energy dealing with sexual harassment it takes time and energy away from the job. Sexual harassment often leads to absenteeism and high staff turnover.

If You are an Employer ...

It's up to the employer to provide a discrimination-free workplace. Whether they are aware of sexual harassment or not, employers are responsible for the actions of management and supervisory personnel, and for the harassment by non-supervisory personnel in certain circumstances.

If, for example, an employee is harassed by a fellow employee and the employer knows about it but doesn't intervene, the employer may also be at fault.

Employers can achieve a discrimination-free workplace by:

- establishing a code of conduct
- establishing an anti-harassment policy
- setting up a confidential complaint process for victims of sexual harassment
- making sure all employees know the policy by posting it, putting it in memo form or in the company newsletter
- letting employees know that penalties will follow sexual harassment, including written or verbal reprimands, suspension, and termination
- establishing a monitoring system

If You are a Victim

1. Tell the harasser to stop

    Make it clear to the harasser that the behaviour is unwelcome. Tell them to stop the behaviour immediately. You can do this verbally, in a letter, or both.

2. Tell the harasser's supervisor

   Employers have a responsibility to protect employees from sexual harassment. Complain to the harasser's supervisor. Insist that management take action.

3. Tell your Union

   If there is a union in your workplace, tell your steward about the harassment. File a grievance. Encourage the union to put an anti-sexual harassment clause in the collective agreement.

4. Talk about it

   Often people who are sexually harassed are too embarrassed to tell anyone, or too afraid of the consequences. It helps to talk to a friend, relative or co-worker you trust.

   If you talk about it you may find others in your workplace have also been harassed. If you're willing to speak up, they might be too.

5. Write it down

   When you complain — whether to your supervisor, union, or the Saskatchewan Human Rights Commission — it helps to document your experience. Write down each remark or action. Try to remember the exact words used. Record dates, times, places and the names of witnesses as soon as possible after the event so the details are still fresh in your memory. Sign and date it.

6. Contact the Saskatchewan Human Rights Commission

   Commission staff investigate complaints. Sometimes victims hesitate to complain because they fear retaliation. Any form of retaliation is against the *Code*.

   A monetary award may be made to complainants to compensate for any loss of income, and for humiliation and loss of self-respect.

   Reprinted by permission of the Saskatchewan Human Rights Commission.

APPENDIX
Canadian Legislation

SEXUAL HARASSMENT

Seven of the human rights Acts in Canada specifically prohibit sexual harassment in the workplace: federal, s. 14; Manitoba, s. 19; Ontario, s. 7(2); Quebec, s. 10.l; New Brunswick, s. 7.1; Nova Scotia, s. 5(2); Newfoundland, s. 13. In addition, the *Canada Labour Code*, which governs federal employees in addition to the *Canadian Human Rights Act*, also has some specific requirements for employers.

In the other jurisdictions, harassment is prohibited as a form of discrimination. The Supreme Court of Canada has held that as a form of sex discrimination, sexual harassment does not need to be mentioned separately in the legislation. This reasoning applies to the other forms of harassment as well. Each of the Canadian human rights Acts protects employees from sex discrimination and, therefore, they are all deemed to protect employees from sexual harassment as well.

The wording of the specific prohibitions against sexual harassment varies. For example, the *Canadian Human Rights Act* provides:

s. 14(l) Harassment. It is a discriminatory practice,

    (a) in the provision of goods, services, facilities or accommodation customarily available to the general public,
    (b) in the provision of commercial premises or residential accommodation, or
    (c) in matters related to employment,

to harass an individual on a prohibited ground of discrimination.

(2) Sexual harassment. Without limiting the generality of subsection (1), sexual harassment shall, for the purposes of that subsection, be deemed to be harassment on a prohibited ground of discrimination.

In addition, the CHRA provides that an employer will be liable for discriminatory acts, which would include harassment, by its employees. The section also includes a due diligence defence:

s. 65(1) Acts of employees, etc. Subject to subsection (2), any act or omission committed by an officer, a director, an employee or an agent of any person, association or organization in the course of the employment of the officer, director, employee or agent shall, for the purposes of this Act, be deemed to be an act or omission committed by that person, association or organization.

(2) Exculpation. An act or omission shall not, by virtue of subsection (1), be deemed to be an act or omission committed by a person, association or organization if it is established that the person, association or organization did not consent to the commission of the act or omission and exercised all due diligence to prevent the act or omission from being committed and, subsequently, to mitigate or avoid the effect thereof.

In Manitoba, the *Human Rights Code* includes both a specific prohibition against harassment and a definition:

s. 19(l) Harassment. No person who is responsible for an activity or undertaking to which this Code applies shall

- (a) harass any person who is participating in the activity or undertaking; or
- (b) knowingly permit, or fail to take reasonable steps to terminate, harassment of one person who is participating in the activity or undertaking by another person who is participating in the activity or undertaking.

(2) "Harassment" defined. In this section, "harassment" means

- (a) a course of abusive and unwelcome conduct or comment undertaken or made on the basis of any characteristic referred to in subsection 9(2); or
- (b) a series of objectionable and unwelcome sexual solicitations or advances; or
- (c) a sexual solicitation or advance made by a person who is in a position to confer any benefit on, or deny any benefit to, the recipient of the solicitation or advance, if the person making the solicitation or advance knows or ought reasonably to know that it is unwelcome; or
- (d) a reprisal or threat of reprisal for rejecting a sexual solicitation or advance.

Similarly, the Ontario *Human Rights Code* prohibits sexual harassment and also provides a definition:

s. 7(2) Harassment because of sex in workplaces. Every person who is an employee has a right to freedom from harassment in the workplace because of sex by his or her employer or agent of the employer or by another employee.

. . . . . .

s. 10(l) "harassment" means engaging in a course of vexatious comment or conduct that is known or ought reasonably to be known to be unwelcome.

OTHER FORMS OF HARASSMENT

Five of the human rights Acts specifically include prohibitions against harassment on grounds other than sex. For example, the federal, Manitoba, Newfoundland and Quebec Acts simply state that it is a discriminatory practice to harass an individual on any prohibited ground of discrimination. This extends the prohibition against harassment in the workplace to protecting employees from harassment on all the grounds that those Acts cover.

The Ontario *Human Rights Code* deals with sexual harassment and other types of harassment separately. Section 7(2) above prohibits sexual harassment in the workplace. Section 5(2) extends the protection to cover other types of harassment stating:

> s. 5(2) Harassment in employment. Every person who is an employee has a right to freedom from harassment in the workplace by the employer or agent of the employer or by another employee because of race, ancestry, place of origin, colour, ethnic origin, citizenship, creed, age, record of offences, marital status, family status or handicap.

For some reason, sexual orientation has not been included in this list. It is curious that the *Code* would specifically protect employees from harassment on all the protected grounds except sexual orientation.

In Quebec, the *Charter of human rights and freedoms* provides:

> s. 10.1 No one may harass a person on the basis of any ground mentioned in section 10.

Both the New Brunswick and Nova Scotia Acts prohibit only sexual harassment and do not mention harassment on the other grounds.

The New Brunswick *Human Rights Act* includes a definition and a prohibition against sexual harassment with respect to employers' organizations, trade unions and professional groups. In addition, the Act outlines liability for employers and a potential defence:

> s. 7.1(1) In this section,
>
> "association" means an employers' organization, a trade union, a professional association or a business or trade association;
> "representative" means a person who acts on behalf of an association or another person;
> "sexually harass" means engage in vexatious comment or conduct of a sexual nature that is known or ought reasonably be known to be unwelcome.
>
> (2) No employer, representative of the employer or person employed by the employer shall sexually harass a person employed by the employer or a person seeking employment with the employer.

. . . . .

(6) For the purposes of this section,

    (a) any act committed by an employee or representative of a person shall be deemed to be an act committed by the person if the person did not exercise the diligence appropriate in the circumstances to prevent the commission of the act;

    (b) any act committed by an employee or representative of an association shall be deemed to be an act committed by the association if an officer or director of the association did not exercise the diligence appropriate in the circumstances to prevent the commission of the act;

    (c) any act committed by an officer or director of an association shall be deemed to be an act committed by the association.

The Nova Scotia *Human Rights Act* provides a lengthy definition of sexual harassment:

    s. 3(o) "sexual harassment" means

        (i) vexatious sexual conduct or a course of comment that is known or ought reasonably to be known as unwelcome,

        (ii) a sexual solicitation or advance made to an individual by another individual where the other individual is in a position to confer a benefit on, or deny a benefit to, the individual to whom the solicitation or advance is made, where the individual who makes the solicitation or advance knows or ought reasonably to know that it is unwelcome, or

        (iii) a reprisal or threat of reprisal against an individual for rejecting a sexual solicitation or advance.

The only other reference to sexual harassment in the Act is the briefly worded prohibition:

    s. 5(2) Sexual harassment. No person shall sexually harass an individual.

The Newfoundland *Human Rights Code* defines "harass":

    s. 2(g) "harass" means to engage in a course of vexatious comment or conduct that is known or ought reasonably to be known to be unwelcome.

CANADA LABOUR CODE — SEXUAL HARASSMENT PROVISIONS

Part 3 of the *Canada Labour Code* contains a section on sexual harassment that includes a definition, a prohibition and, as well, mandates the creation of a policy statement, the contents of which are outlined in some detail. This is the only labour relations legislation in Canada that contains such a provision.

Part 3 of the *Code* sets out employment standards for employees in the federal jurisdiction and relates primarily to the non-union sector. It is, however, interesting to note it as an example of a statutory response to the problem of workplace sexual harassment found outside of human rights legislation:

Definition of "sexual harassment"

247.1 In this Division, "sexual harassment" means any conduct, comment, gesture or contact of a sexual nature:

- (a) that is likely to cause offence or humiliation to any employee; or
- (b) that might, on reasonable grounds, be perceived by that employee as placing a condition of a sexual nature on employment or on any opportunity for training or promotion.

Right of employee

247.2 Every employee is entitled to employment free of sexual harassment.

Responsibility of employer

247.3 Every employer shall make every reasonable effort to ensure that no employee is subjected to sexual harassment.

Policy statement by employer

247.4(1) Every employer shall, after consulting with the employees or their representatives, if any, issue a policy statement concerning sexual harassment.

(2) The policy statement required by subsection (1) may contain any term consistent with the tenor of this Division the employer considers appropriate but must contain the following:

- (a) a definition of sexual harassment that is substantially the same as the definition in section 247.1;
- (b) a statement to the effect that every employee is entitled to employment free of sexual harassment;
- (c) a statement to the effect that the employer will make every reasonable effort to ensure that no employee is subjected to sexual harassment;
- (d) a statement to the effect that the employer will take such disciplinary measures as the employer deems appropriate against any person under the employer's direction who subjects any employee to sexual harassment;
- (e) a statement explaining how complaints of sexual harassment may be brought to the attention of the employer;
- (f) a statement to the effect that the employer will not disclose the name of a complainant or the circumstances related to the complaint to any person except where disclosure is necessary for

the purposes of investigating the complaint or taking disciplinary measures in relation thereto; and

(g) a statement informing employees of the discriminatory practices provisions of the *Canadian Human Rights Act* that pertain to rights of persons to seek redress under that Act in respect of sexual harassment.

Publicity

(3) Every employer shall make each person under the employer's direction aware of the policy statement required by subsection (1).

References

Alberta Human Rights Commission. "Developing and Creating an Effective Sexual Harassment Policy".

Alberta Human Rights Commission. "Sample Sexual Harassment Policy".

Alberta Human Rights Commission. "Sexual Harassment".

B.C. Hydro. "Harassment Free — A Guide to Creating a Respectful Workplace" (1994).

British Columbia Council of Human Rights (now British Columbia Human Rights Commission). "Sexual Harassment and Human Rights".

The Canadian Bar Association. "Touchstones for Change — Equality, Diversity and Accountability, Report of The Canadian Bar Association Task Force on Gender Equality in the Legal Profession" (Ottawa, 1993).

Canadian Human Rights Commission. "A Guide to Screening and Selection in Employment" (Ottawa: Ministry of Supply and Services Canada, 1993).

Canadian Human Rights Commission. "Harassment Casebook — Summaries of Selected Harassment Cases" (Ottawa: Ministry of Supply and Services Canada, 1993).

Canadian Human Rights Commission. "Harassment — What It Is and What To Do About It" (Ottawa: Ministry of Supply and Services Canada, 1993).

Canadian Institute of Actuaries. "Guidelines on the Avoidance of Sexual Stereotyping within the Canadian Institute of Actuaries" (Ottawa, 1993).

Canadian Union of Public Employees. "The Fact Sheet — Workplace Harassment", Wishart, C.

Community Legal Information Association of P.E.I. Inc. "Sexual Harassment", Larkin, I. (December 1992).

Manitoba Human Rights Commission. "Fact Sheet: Prohibiting Harassment" (effective April 18, 1988).

Manitoba Human Rights Commission. "Sexual Harassment — Rights and Responsibilities" (revised January 1995).

New Brunswick Human Rights Commission. "Sexual Harassment in Employment" (March 1993).

Newfoundland Human Rights Commission. "Sexual Harassment in the Workplace — An Information Guide for Employees and Employers".

Nova Scotia Human Rights Commission. "Human Rights — What is Racial Harassment?".

Nova Scotia Human Rights Commission. "Human Rights — What is Sexual Harassment?".

Ontario Human Rights Commission. "Policy Statement on Racial Slurs and Harassment and Racial Jokes" (Queen's Printer for Ontario, 1994).

Parliamentary Committee on Equality Rights. "Equality for All" (Ottawa, 1985).

Saskatchewan Human Rights Commission. "Sexual Harassment" (revised June 1994).

Saskatchewan Human Rights Commission. "Erasing Racism".

Saskatchewan Women's Secretariat. "Preventing Harassment — A Guide for Employers".

Index

B.C. HYDRO POLICY
identifying harassment, 55-56
preventing harassment, 56, 58
   employees, 56
   supervisors and managers, 58
workplace harassment policy, 77, 81-89

BUSINESS TRIPS
"course of employment", whether in, 30-31
   criteria, 30
personal nature, whether activities of, 31
work-related conferences, 29-31

COMPANIES
corporate liability, 48-49
responsible if do not respond appropriately to complaints, 49-51
responsible for providing workplace free of harassment, 49

COMPLAINT
complaint procedure, 74, 93, 122
dealing with, 91-92, 94
handling
   formal complaints, 94, 96
   informal complaints, 95-96

investigation of,
   documenting findings in report, 111-112
   guidelines for conducting, 96-98
   how to receive, 104-107
      what, where and when, 105-107
      who, 74, 104-105
         designated employees, 68, 74-75, 93, 104-105, 107-108
         important qualities, 104-105
   investigation plan, developing, 107-108
   investigation protocol, 108-111
      confidentiality, 75, 94, 109-110
   joint, 99
   why investigate, 103-104. See also **RESPONSIBILITY AND CONSEQUENCES**

CO-WORKERS
behaviour, harassing, 23-24
goal at each workplace, 24
impact of inability to communicate, 24
negative working conditions, 24

CUSTOMERS AND CLIENTS
generally, 25-26
obligations of employer, 26-27

FLIRTATION AND DATING
questions and answers regarding, 37-38
social and sexual relationship distinguished from sexual harassment, 38-41
   abuse of power, whether use or, 38
   between employee and manager, 38-41

GENDER HARASSMENT
case law, 7-8, 50
C.B.A. Task Force on Gender Equality in the Legal Profession, 8-9
generally, 7, 9
jokes and comments, 42

"HARASSMENT" DEFINED
age harassment, 17-18
behaviour, harassing, 1-3
   self-test, 2
examples, typical, 35-36
gender harassment, 7-9
   case law, 7-8
   C.B.A. Task Force on Gender Equality in the Legal Profession, 8-9
   generally, 7, 9
Manitoba Human Rights Code, 1, 71-72, 138
mental and physical disability harassment, 13-15
   employees with mental disabilities, 13-14
   employees with physical disabilities, 14-15
   generally, 15

human rights legislation, 13
New Brunswick, 71
Newfoundland Human Rights Code, 3-4, 71, 140
Ontario Human Rights Code, 1, 71, 137-139
personal harassment, 18
Quebec Charter of human rights and freedoms, 139
racial harassment, 10-13
   behaviour, harassing, 10-11
   directed at another person, 11
   generally, 10, 13
   impact, devastating, 11
   jury selection decision of Ontario Court of Appeal, 10
   Policy Statement on Racial Slurs and Harassment and Racial Jokes, 12
religious harassment, 15-16
   verbal abuse, joking or taunting, 16
sexual harassment, 3-7. See also **SEXUAL HARASSMENT**
   British Columbia, 4
   Canada Labour Code, 4, 71, 137, 140-142
   Canadian Human Rights Act, 137-138
   case law, 4-7
   common elements, 4-6
   examples, typical, 36
   male victims, 6-7
   Manitoba Human Rights Code, 1, 71-72, 137, 138
   New Brunswick Human Rights Act, 137, 139-140
   Newfoundland, 3-4, 137, 139-140
   Nova Scotia Human Rights Act, 3, 71, 137, 139, 140
   Ontario Human Rights Code, 1, 137, 138

prohibited as form of
discrimination, 137-139
Quebec Charter of human
rights and freedoms, 137,
139
Supreme Court of Canada, 5,
72-73
sexual orientation harassment, 16-
17, 139

**HARASSMENT, TYPICAL
EXAMPLES OF**
flirtation and dating, 37
questions and answers
regarding, 37-38
social or sexual relationship
distinguished from sexual
harassment, 38-41
abuse of power, whether
use or, 38
between employee and
manager, 38-40
whether sexual conduct
was unwelcome, 40-41
two criteria, 40-41
harassment in general, 35-36
jokes and comments, 41-43
generally, 41-42
racial harassment, 10-11
Policy Statement on Racial
Slurs and Harassment and
Racial Jokes, 12
posters, calendars and pictures, 43
sexual harassment, 36

**HUMAN RIGHTS
COMMISSIONS**
publications
Alberta Human Rights
Commission
sexual harassment policy,
90-92, 115-118

British Columbia Human
Rights Commission
sexual harassment, 118-
123
Canadian Human Rights
Commission
preventing harassment, 61-
62
sexual harassment, 113-
115
Manitoba Human Rights
Commission
preventing harassment, 60,
123-125
New Brunswick Human
Rights Commission
preventing harassment, 60,
126-127
sexual harassment, 125-
128
Newfoundland Human Rights
Commission
harassed employees, 65
preventing harassment, 61
sexual harassment, 128-
130
Nova Scotia Human Rights
Commission
sexual harassment, 130-
131
Prince Edward Island,
Community Legal
Information Association of,
harassed employees, 64-65
sexual harassment, 131-
133
Saskatchewan Human Rights
Commission
erasing racism, 56-57
preventing harassment, 59-
60
sexual harassment, 133-
136

INVESTIGATION OF COMPLAINT. See **COMPLAINT**

JOB APPLICANTS
generally, 19
guide to screening and selection in employment, 19-23
    disability, 21-22
    race, 21
    religion, 21
    sexual orientation, 22
irrelevant personal information, consequences of request for, 23

JOKES AND COMMENTS
Canadian Human Rights Commission
    preventing harassment, 61-62
corporate liability, 48-49
gender harassment, 42
generally, 41-42
racial harassment, 10-11
    Policy Statement on Racial Slurs and Harassment and Racial Jokes, 12
sexual harassment, 42-43

MANAGERS. See **SUPERVISORS AND MANAGERS**

MENTAL AND PHYSICAL DISABILITY HARASSMENT
employees with mental disabilities, 13-14, 46-47
employees with physical disabilities, 14-15
generally, 15
human rights legislation, 13

OFFICE PARTIES
course of employment, 32
scope of employment, whether within, 31-32
    criteria, 31-32
    "spill over" effect, 32

POSTERS, CALENDARS AND PICTURES
Canadian Human Rights Commission
    preventing harassment, 61-62
generally, 43

PREVENTING HARASSMENT. See **STEPS THAT CAN BE TAKEN**

RACIAL HARASSMENT
behaviour, harassing, 10-11
directed at another person, 11
erasing racism, 56-57
generally, 10, 11
impact, devastating, 11
jury selection decision of Ontario Court of Appeal, 10
Policy Statement on Racial Slurs and Harassment and Racial Jokes, 12
responsibility of employer, 51

RESPONSIBILITY AND CONSEQUENCES
companies, 48-51
    corporate liability, 48-50
        responsible for providing workplace free of harassment, 49, 50
        responsible if do not respond appropriately to complaints, 49-51
    senior manager jointly liable with company, 50-51

conclusion, 53
disciplinary options, range of, 45
human rights commissions
  guidelines
    Alberta, 51-52
    Manitoba, 52
    New Brunswick, 52
    Newfoundland, 53
    Nova Scotia, 52-53
supervisors and managers, 46-47, 50
  active harassment, 46-47
  allowing atmosphere of harassment, 47
termination and wrongful dismissal, 45-46
unions, 47-48
  intra-union disputes involving harassment, 48
  non-discriminatory workplaces, 47-48
workplace harassment policy, 45

SEXUAL HARASSMENT
Alberta Human Rights Commission
  guidelines, 51-52
  sexual harassment policy, 90-92, 115-118
B.C. Hydro policy, 77, 84-85
British Columbia, 4
British Columbia Human Rights Commission, 118-123
Canada Labour Code, 4, 69-70, 72, 137, 140-142
Canadian Human Rights Act, 137-138
Canadian Human Rights Commission, 113-115
case law, 4-7
common elements, 4-6
gender harassment, 7-9
generally, 3-7
harassed employees
  steps that can be taken, 63-65
male victims, 6-7
Manitoba Human Rights Code, 1, 137, 138
Manitoba Human Rights Commission, 123-125
New Brunswick, 137, 139-140
  liability for employers, 52, 139-140
  preventing harassment, 60
New Brunswick Human Rights Commission, 125-128
  preventing harassment, 52, 60
  sexual harassment, 125-128
Newfoundland, 3-4, 137
  preventing harassment, 61
  sexual harassment, 128-130
Nova Scotia, 3, 137, 139, 140
Nova Scotia Human Rights Commission
  reasons for preventing harassment, 52-53
  sexual harassment, 130-131
Ontario Human Rights Code, 1, 137-139
Prince Edward Island, 131-133
Quebec, 137
Saskatchewan Human Rights Commission
  preventing harassment, 59-60
  sexual harassment, 133-136
Saskatchewan Women's Secretariat
  sample policy on harassment, 92-98
Supreme Court of Canada, 5
typical examples, 36

SOCIAL ACTIVITIES, AFTER-HOURS
"personal in nature", 32

scope of employment duties,
whether within, 32-33
criteria, 32-33
"spill over" effect, 33

STEPS THAT CAN BE TAKEN
steps that employers can take, 58-63
    human rights commissions' advice on preventing harassment, 59-62
        Canadian, 61-62
        Manitoba, 60
        New Brunswick, 60
        Saskatchewan, 59-60
    training sessions, designing, 65-68
        factors, 65-67
        three levels, 67-68
            designated employees, 68
            employee sessions, 67
            supervisor and manager training, 67-68
    unwritten rules of workplace, 59
    workplace harassment policy. See also **WORKPLACE HARASSMENT POLICY**
        drafting, 62
        generally 58-59
        publishing, 62
        training, 63
steps that harassed employees can take, 63-65
    New Brunswick, 63-64
    Newfoundland, 65
    Prince Edward Island, 64
    Saskatchewan, 63
steps that individual employees can take, 55-57
    conclusion, 57
    erasing racial harassment, 56-57
    identifying harassing behaviour, 55-56
    preventing harassment, 56
steps that supervisors and managers can take, 58
    preventing harassment, 58

SUPERVISORS AND MANAGERS
preventing harassment, 58
responsibility and consequences, 46-47, 50
    active harassment, 46-47
    allowing atmosphere of harassment, 47
social or sexual relationship distinguished from sexual harassment, 39-41
    whether sexual conduct was unwelcome, 40-41
source of harassment, 25
training sessions, 67-68
workplace harassment policy, 25

TRAINING SESSIONS. See also **STEPS THAT CAN BE TAKEN**
designing, 65-68
    factors, 65-67
    three levels, 67-68
        designated employees, 68
        employee sessions, 67
        supervisor and manager training, 67-68
potential consequences, 76

UNIONS
collective agreement clauses (C.U.P.E.)
    workplace harassment, 98-101

intra-union disputes involving harassment, 48
non-discriminatory workplaces, 47-48
workplace harassment policy (more than 1000 employees), 81-89

WORKPLACE HARASSMENT POLICY
application (fourth element), 74
basic elements, 69, 77
confidentiality (seventh element), 75
definition (second element), 71-73
    Canada Labour Code, 72
    generally, 71
    Manitoba, 71-72
    Nova Scotia, 72
    Supreme Court of Canada, 72-73
examples (third element), 73
federally regulated company, 69-70
    policy statement on sexual harassment, 69-70
general statement (first element), 70-71
introduction, 77
large corporation: union environment (more than 1000 employees), 81-89
medium-sized corporation: non-union environment (about 1000 employees), 80-81
penalties (tenth element), 76
process (sixth element), 74-75
prohibition of retribution (eighth element), 75-76
remedies (ninth element), 76
sample policy on harassment (Saskatchewan Women's Secretariat), 92-98
sample sexual harassment policy (Alberta), 90-92
small professional firm (under 100 employees), 78-79
union clauses
    workplace harassment, 98-101
who receives complaints (fifth element), 74

WORKPLACE, SCOPE OF, 29